KU-242-095

THE STORY BEGINS

Also by Amos Oz

AMOS OZ

The Story Begins
Essays on Literature

Translated by Maggie Bar-Tura

Chatto & Windus
LONDON

Published by Chatto & Windus 1999

2 4 6 8 10 9 7 5 3 1

First published in Hebrew as *Matchilim Sipur*
Jerusalem 1996

English edition first published in the United States in 1999 by
Harcourt Brace & Company, New York

First published in Great Britain in 1999 by
Chatto & Windus
Random House, 20 Vauxhall Bridge Road, London SW1V 2SA

Random House Australia (Pty) Limited
20 Alfred Street, Milsons Point, Sydney,
New South Wales 2061, Australia

Random House New Zealand Limited
18 Poland Road, Glenfield,
Auckland 10, New Zealand

Random House South Africa (Pty) Limited
Endulini, 5A Jubilee Road, Parktown 2193, South Africa

Random House UK Limited Reg. No. 954009

A CIP catalogue record for this book is available from the British Library

ISBN 0 7011 6883 8

Printed and bound in Great Britain by
Biddles Ltd, Guildford and King's Lynn

Contents

CONTENTS

The Story Begins

Introduction

But What Actually Existed Here Before the Big Bang?

My father wrote scholarly books. He always envied me my novelist's freedom to write as I wish, straight from my head onto the page, unconfined by all kinds of preliminary search and research, unburdened by the obligation to acquaint myself with all existing data in the field, unharnessed from the yoke of comparing sources, providing evidence, checking quotations and installing footnotes: free as a bird. You have the itch to write "Shmuel loves Tsila"? You just go ahead and write it. You wish to write "but Tsila loves Gilbert"? Off you go. You wish to add "nonetheless, Shmuel and Gilbert love each other?" Who can refute you? Who can come up and challenge you with contradicting data or with sources you might have overlooked?

I, on the other hand, harbored a certain envy of my father. Each time he sat down to work on an academic paper, his desk was crowded, edge to edge, with open books, offprints, references, lexicons, a battery of supporting artillery. He never had to sit, as I do, staring at a single mocking blank page in the middle of an arid desk, like a crater on the face of the moon. Just me and emptiness and despair. Go make something out of nothing at all. By the way, I am talking about the same desk. When my father died, I inherited his desk, which for years and years was heavily populated, like a Calcutta slum, whereas now it is as deserted as the Kosovo airstrip.

Actually, who hasn't been through the ghastly experience of sitting in front of a blank page, with its toothless mouth grinning at you: Go ahead, let's see you lay a finger on me?

A blank page is actually a whitewashed wall with no door and no window. Beginning to tell a story is like making a pass at a total stranger in a restaurant. Remember Chekhov's Gurov in "The Lady with the Dog"? Gurov beckons to the little dog, wagging his finger at it over and over again, until the lady says, blushing, "He doesn't bite," whereupon Gurov asks her permission to give the dog a bone. Both Gurov and Chekhov have now been given a thread to go by; the flirtation begins and the story takes off.

The beginning of almost every story is actually a bone, something with which to court the dog, which may bring you closer to the lady.

Imagine you decide to write about a girl from Nahariya—let's call her Mathilda—who finds out that she has an unknown cousin in Greece. Suppose the cousin is also named Mathilda. Fancy that Mathilda from Nahariya decides to go to Greece in September to meet her namesake cousin. Very well, but what should come first? Mathilda waking up one bright morning? Mathilda at the travel agency? Mathilda as a little girl, on that memorable day when her fingers got caught in the ventilator? Or Mathilda in Thessalonika, renting a room in a hotel crowded with farmers, where she meets a shy beekeeper? Or should we, perhaps, begin the story with a detailed description of the thick cobwebs in the storeroom beneath the staircase? What goes into the first chapter? Mathilda staring at the earrings that used to belong to her great-grandmother, whose name was also Mathilda? And what should be on the first page? In the opening paragraph? How much should the first sentence reveal? "Midway in our life's journey, I went astray / from the straight road and woke to find myself / alone in a dark wood"? (Dante's *Inferno*.) Perhaps Dante's opening stanza for the *Inferno* could serve as a standard opening line for all stories: 'Midway in our life's journey' is, more or less, where so many stories actually begin.

So, you sit down and ask yourself what should come first; how to get to that midway debut? Sitting. Scribbling on the page. Crumpling it. Throwing it away. Scribbling on the next page: shapes, flowers, triangles, rhombuses, a house with a little chimney, a bald cat. Crumpling again. Throwing it away. By now Mathilda begins to fade away. You turn over a new leaf. Alas, the new leaf isn't any friendlier than the previous one. That's the way it is: no dog—no lady.

Actually, this happens all the time, not just to novelists but to anyone who writes down anything at all. Tsila was commissioned to interview Gilbert, one of the applicants for the position of staff coordinator in a manufacturing plant. Tsila is expected to report her impression in writing. She writes, "The interview took place in the Café Baghdad at 6 P.M."

She crosses it out. This is not quite right, because the

3

interview had indeed begun at 6 P.M. but took place between 6 and 6:45. Besides, who cares if it was 6 or 8, Baghdad or Alaska? She crosses it out again. Bites the tip of her pen. Thinks. Then she writes, "In the beginning of the interview, Gilbert provided me with. . . ." Crosses it out again; replaces "Gilbert" with "the applicant provided me with a CV, which he insisted I read then and there, before we started our conversation. The CV is enclosed."

Crosses it out. What difference does it make? Besides, "insisted" is too strong here, for Gilbert was actually less decisive than that. "Asked"? Too weak. In fact, he less than insisted but more than asked that I read his CV first. Is there a word halfway between "asked" and "insisted"? Perhaps "required"? No, he had not required. And he was not "decisive." All in all, "decisive" is such a silly word. In any case, the CV is going to be attached to my report, if I ever manage to write it, so who cares whether Gilbert insisted, persisted, asked, begged or tempted me? (Tempted me? Gilbert? What has got into you, Tsila, all of a sudden?) Well, perhaps it can be written this way, "The applicant gave me the impression that he was a man of extraordinary self-confidence, even though he might have been a touch too deliberate in trying to give this impression." Fine, except actually it stinks: he gave the impression that he was deliberately "trying to give this impression." Lousy logic, and lousy Hebrew as well. Besides, "extraordinary self-confidence"—who do you think you are? A certified assessor of self-confidence?

Tsila starts over again: "Gilbert Kadosh, 29, born in Gedera, Israel, divorced, served for five years as a police inspector. . . ." No. Hell, can't you even get your facts straight? He did serve with the police force for five years, but he was an inspector for only the last year and a half.

4

And why not start with the zest of it? But what in the world *is* the zest of it? Besides, it's getting late. And Tsila promised to call Mathilda before the end of her shift.

Lousy again. It's not clear whether "her shift" refers to Mathilda's shift or to Tsila's.

Enough. Tsila will not produce this report today. Tomorrow is another day. This is not the end of the world.

Crosses it out again. "Tomorrow is another day" is so trite. On the other hand, so what? What's wrong with something trite? Why not? And isn't it rather clumsy to conclude with three synonymous questions, "So what? What's wrong? Why not?"

Tsila tears her draft to pieces and calls Mathilda (who had gone to Greece to look for that other Mathilda).

It is hard to begin.

True, there are various strategies to deal with this hardship: some writers never start from the word go, but, rather, with a couple of easy scenes from the middle of their story, just to warm up their fingers. (The trouble is that even an easy scene from the middle of the story needs an opening sentence.) Some, like Camus's Grand in *The Plague,* write and rewrite the first sentence of a book a hundred times and never get beyond it. Other writers, presumably, give up altogether and, perhaps in despair or exhausted, decide to begin just as it comes to them, what the hell is the difference, one can start off wherever, with anything at all, even with something flat or slightly silly. Here, for example, is the great Dostoyevsky himself in his poor beginning to a story called "White Nights": "It was a lovely night, one of those nights, dear reader, which can only happen when you are young. The sky was so bright and starry that when you looked at it the first question that came into your mind was whether it was really possible that all sorts of bad-tempered and un-stable people could live under such a glorious sky."

Well, quite embarrassing. Even the toady appeal to "dear reader" cannot redeem this from its sentimental banality. And this, after all, is none other than Dostoyev-sky. God knows how many drafts upon drafts he made, re-wrote, destroyed, cursed, scribbled, crumpled, threw onto the fire, drowned in the lavatory, before finally settling for this sort of "so be it."

Or maybe not so. After all, "White Nights" is a story written in the first person from the point of view of a sentimental character, and its subtitle is "A Sentimental Love Story (From the Memories of a Dreamer)." So the miserable opening sentence may well be deliberately, premeditatedly miserable.

If so, our question must be reopened. How many drafts did Dostoyevsky have to write and rewrite before finally achieving this rare specimen of a poor opening sentence? How much refinement and distilling went into that star-seeded sky, that "dear reader" and that "only happen when you are young"? In other words, were the emperor's new clothes in Andersen's fairy tale truly no more than a sheer fraud, meant to expose the emperor's folly and the crowd's conformism? Or perhaps the brave boy who shouted "He doesn't have anything on" was also a fool, albeit a fool in a different league? Could it be that the naked emperor was really not naked at all but wonderfully garbed, and the crooked tailor was no fraud but an amazing master whose genius might have been way above the grasp of the crowd, way above the comprehension of the emperor, way above the range of the boy? Is it not feasible that only the subtlest viewers could have noticed the splendor of the emperor's new clothes, the beauty of which evaded the emperor, the mob, even the daring deconstructionist boy, who must have searched all the archives before exposing the emperor's nakedness, not because the emperor was any more naked than other emperors—or other human beings—but precisely because naked emperors are, today, the special bargain of the week?

One could put the question as follows: Where, if anywhere at all, is the line between presenting a sentimental character in the first person and producing a sentimental text? Or are there no longer good and bad texts, but only legitimate, well-received texts and other texts, no less legitimate, deprived of a good reception?

Back to our dilemma. Where does a story properly begin? Any beginning of a story is always a kind of contract between writer and reader. There are, of course, all sorts of contracts, including those that are insincere. Sometimes the opening paragraph or chapter works like a secret pact between writer and reader, behind the protagonist's back. This is the case at the beginning of *Don Quixote* and of Agnon's *Just Yesterday*. There are deceitful contracts, where the writer seems to reveal all kinds of secrets, so that the unsuspecting reader takes the bait, imagining that he is actually invited to enter the dark room, failing to realize that "backstage" is not really behind the scenery but just a second set; while the reader fancies that he is a part of a conspiracy, he is actually no more than the victim of a subtler conspiracy: the visible contract is no more than a make-believe object, the subject of an inner, subtler, more devious contract. Such, for instance, is the case in the beginning of Kleist's *Michael Kohlhaas,* of Kafka's *The Trial,* and of Thomas Mann's *The Chosen.* (The first chapter of *The Chosen* is entitled "Who Tolls the Bells?"

and the reader is earnestly informed that it is not the bell-ringer who tolls the bell but "the spirit of the story," only to find out later that this spirit-of-the-story is actually no spirit but an Irishman named Clemence.)

There are beginnings that work rather like a honey trap: at first you are seduced with a juicy piece of gossip, or an all-revealing confession, or a bloodcurdling adventure, but eventually you find out that what you are getting is not a fish, but a stuffed fish. In *Moby-Dick,* for example, there are many adventures, but also many delicatessen items not mentioned on the menu, not even hinted at in the opening contract ("Call me Ishmael"), but conferred upon you as a special bonus—as though you bought an ice cream and won a ticket to travel around the world.

There are philosophical contracts, such as the famous first sentence of Tolstoy's *Anna Karenina:* "All happy families resemble one another; every unhappy family is unhappy in its own fashion." Actually, Tolstoy himself, in *Anna Karenina* and in other works, contradicts this dichotomy.

Sometimes we are confronted with a harsh opening contract, almost forbidding, which warns the reader right from the outset: Tickets are very expensive here. If you feel you cannot afford a tough advance payment, you'd better not even try to get in. No concessions and no discounts are to be expected. Such, for instance, is the beginning of Faulkner's *The Sound and the Fury.*

But what, ultimately, *is* a beginning? Can there exist, in principle, a proper beginning to any story at all? Isn't there always, without exception, a latent beginning-before-the-beginning? A forward to the introduction to the prologue? A pre–Genesis occurrence? A reason for the motif for the factor from which the initial cause originated? Edward A. Said has distinguished between "origin" (a passive being) and "beginning" (which he regards as an active concept).* If, for instance, we wish to begin a story with the sentence "Gilbert was born in Gedera the day after the storm that uprooted the chinaberry tree and destroyed the fence," we may still have to tell about the falling of the chinaberry tree, perhaps even about its planting, or we might have to go back to when, from where, and why Gilbert's parents came to Gedera, of all places, and why Gedera was settled, and where the fallen fence was. For if Gilbert Kadosh was born, someone must have taken the trouble to beget him; someone must have hoped for something; or feared, loved or not loved. Someone

---

* Edward A. Said, *Beginnings: Intentions and Methods;* Johns Hopkins University Press, Baltimore and London, 1978, 6. Said's study is devoted primarily to the theory of criticism, offering perspectives on the European novel, analyzing the meaning of "beginning." According to Said, a beginning is, essentially, an act of returning, of going back, and not just a departure point for linear progress. "Beginning and beginning anew," he argues, "are historical matters, whereas 'origin' is divine." In each and every beginning there are intention and attitude. Every beginning creates uniqueness but also weaves the existing, the known, into the heritage of language creation of humankind along with its own fruitful and unique removal. In Said's view, each beginning is actually an interplay between the familiar and the new (Introduction, 13). On the primeval relationship between beginning, creation and solitude, see also Penelope Farmer's introduction to her anthology of myths of creation, *Beginnings: Creation Myths of the World;* Chatto and Windus, London, 1978, 3–4. Concerning the significance of the departure point for a story, see also Leah Goldberg, *The Unity of the Human Being and the Universe in Tolstoy;* Y. L. Magnes Publishing House, Jerusalem, 1959, Hebrew. I also heard interesting thoughts about beginnings of certain Hebrew stories and novels many years ago in a conversation with the late Shlomo Grodjensky. Shulamit Hareven deals with the beginnings of stories in her fine essay "All the Beginnings," included in her collection *Ivrim b'Aza (Blind in Gaza);* Amudim L'Sifrut Ivrit and Zemora-Bitan Ltd. Tel Aviv, 1991, Hebrew, 172–178.

9

asked and had been granted; someone enjoyed, or just pretended to enjoy. In short, if the story is to live up to its ideal duty, it must go back at least all the way to the Big Bang, that cosmic orgasm with which, presumably, all smaller bangs began. And by the way, what actually existed here just before the Big Bang? A former incarnation of Gedera?

In our opening contract, the one with the storm and the chinaberry tree, there ought to exist, like a chromosome, that which will one day make Gilbert Kadosh marry, then divorce, enroll in the police force, then retire and apply for a new job, which is what brought about his meeting with Tsila, when he asked—insisted; no, neither asked nor insisted, but something between insist and ask— and ever since he did, Tsila has been fascinated by him, eventually finding out that Shmuel, who loves her, is also falling in love with Gilbert.

Or should we not begin with Gilbert or Tsila, but with this Shmuel? Or even with Shmuel's great-grandmother, Mathilda, who was also the great-grandmother of Tsila's friend Mathilda, the one who went to Greece to look for her unknown namesake cousin?

This book is based on my teachings at Kibbutz Hulda's high school, at the Brenner Regional High School, at Ben Gurion University of the Negev, at Boston University, and also on a series of lectures delivered in the Eretz Yisrael Museum in Tel Aviv in 1995–1996.

—AMOS OZ,
Arad, 1996

The Imperceptible Progress of Shade

On the Beginning of Effi Briest
by Theodore Fontane

Theodore Fontane's novel *Effi Briest* was published in
1894; Nili Mirsky's Hebrew translation, which I
read, appeared in 1981. *Effi Briest* is the story of a young
woman in Prussia, daughter of a respected and well-to-do
family, whose parents have married her to the noble Baron
von Innstetten, an older man and an army officer. Years
before the story begins, there was an unfulfilled love affair
between the Baron and Effi's mother. The match is a
desirable one between two respectable families, yet the
partners are ill-suited to each other: Effi is spontaneous,
emotional and temperamental; her husband, Innstetten, is
a reserved, logical, decent and considerate man who cares
for his young wife in his own cautious fashion. He is not
unlike Alexei Alexandrovitch Karenin in Tolstoy's *Anna
Karenina* (although the Prussian noble is less fossilized
than the senior Russian official, and his ears are apparently much smaller than Karenin's). The strict values of

11

the Prussian upper class play a central role in the novel. They are values of duty, honor, obedience and discipline, strict routine and emotional restraint.

While Innstetten is traveling, Effi engages in an affair with Major Crampas, a whiskered womanizer and gambler, a clever Don Juan, "a ladies' man." When the affair becomes known to the Baron, he, of course, challenges the lover to a duel, in which the husband successfully overcomes and kills his opponent.

Effi is banished from the house, at first to an isolated apartment. She is separated from her only daughter, Annie, in order to punish her for her crime of adultery and to remove the child from her mother's immoral influence. Young Annie remains with her father, the Baron, who educates her according to the values of honor and tradition. Effi Briest is a distant literary relative of Anna Karenina and of Emma Bovary, and has perhaps one or two things in common with Tirtza in Agnon's "In the Prime of Her Life." Toward the end of the story, Effi returns to her parents' home, where she finds a kind of serenity, resulting from a deep kind of acceptance. Some time later she dies, in the house where she was born and raised, the very house whose exterior is described in the beginning of the novel. A fleeting glance at the story's beginning reveals only a still, unpeopled world. More precisely: an almost inanimate world. And even more precisely: still objects imposing stillness.

In front of the von Briests' house in Hohen-Cremmen— their family house since the reign of the Elector George Willhelm—the village street lay bathed in the glare of the midday sun, whilst towards the park and gardens, a side-wing, built on at right angles, cast a broad shadow, first on a white and green flagged path and, beyond, on a large round flower-bed with a sundial in the middle and cannas and rhubarb growing round its edge. A dozen yards further on, exactly symmetrical with the wing, ran a churchyard wall with small-leafed ivy growing along its whole length except where it was pierced by a small, white-painted iron gate; beyond the wall rose the tall tower of Hohen-Cremmen, with its shingle roof and its glittering, recently regilded weather-cock.

The house, the wing and the churchyard wall formed a horseshoe enclosing a small ornamental garden, open on one side to reveal a little lake and a jetty to which a boat was moored and, close by, a swing with its wooden seat suspended from two ropes at each end; the posts supporting the wooden crossbar were already somewhat askew. Between the lake and the circular bed, however, half hiding the swing, stood a few immense old plane trees.

Is this not a tourist's picture postcard? A saccharine landscape of the sort once placed in living rooms, above the piano, to match the armchairs and the crystal chandeliers, to give the room an atmosphere of wealth, elegance and comfort? In any event, this is a very slow and quiet description, the like of which is no longer to be found in contemporary prose, and for which contemporary readers may have no taste or patience, and it may arouse a certain impatient shrug from a reader who comes to it directly from Raymond Carver. The reader who looks for a serpentine plot will not find it here. *Effi Briest* is a lily in almost still waters. Of all the forms of narrative prose, the novel is best equipped to render the tiny, microscopic trajectory, the deviations, which cause an entire life to shift slowly from its course, going astray and ending in disappointment.

Careful reading reveals that the tranquillity of the opening section is tense and the harmony in the scene is under threat: the village street stretches in front of the house, both enveloped with serenity and flooded with light. Unlike the street, the park and the garden lie in shadow, but this shade is dynamic, not static: the shade of the wing falls at first on the flagged path, and from there it advances toward the circular flower bed. Behind the flower bed stands the wall of the churchyard, which, like the street, stretches.

Not just the lines of shade, from the path to the flower bed, but almost everything here is fashioned with geometric severity: the wing meets the main house at a right angle; the path is paved with green and white tiles; the flower bed is round, with a sundial stuck in its navel and decorative edging; the churchyard wall is parallel to the wing. And beyond all this, a tower rises. Buildings and wall enclose the garden in a "horseshoe." We are even told that the swing is made of a horizontal wooden seat hanging by two ropes from a wooden crossbar resting on posts that are not straight. The painting is thus geometric, almost cubist.

The sense of extended observation, the trickle of slow-moving time, is achieved here by a hint of movement of the shadows, which is by nature continuous, from the tiled path to the round flower bed: a quick glance could not take in the crawl of the shadows, from which we understand that the observation of the buildings and the garden is an ongoing activity, and that the observer is stationary, that his viewpoint is unchanging. There is also a hinted presence of other movements, which have been blocked or frozen: the swing, the pond, the boat tied to the jetty. The churchyard wall is described here as "exactly symmetrical" with the wing: but this symmetry becomes claustrophobic and oppressing. We are told that there is an opening in the wall, only one; then we learn that it is not a door, but a white iron gate, and that it is "small." Thus grows a feeling of prison, an atmosphere of claustrophobia, even before we learn that the prisoner is "a small ornamental garden" enclosed by three heavy inanimate bodies: the massive house, the right-angled wing and the churchyard wall, which has only a small gate. At the open end of the horseshoe, although there is a small lake with a boat in it, the boat is tied to the jetty. Finally we discover that the open side, which allows eye contact from the flower bed to the lake, is also, in effect, blocked: between the lake and the circular flower bed stood several huge old plane trees, which almost hid the swing.

And so we have a young woman, Effi Briest, and her world, which has closed around her, depicted here even before the appearance of the character, the social background, the period, the prohibitions and the failed attempt to break out.

The weathervane rooster at the top of the tower is not new. Perhaps the rooster, like the house of the noble von Briests, stands there from the days of Elector George Willhelm. Only its gold leaf is new and shiny. The entire picture expresses strength and stability, the accumulated power of many generations, strict order, authority, severity. But this is a fortress threatened from within: the leaning posts of the swing, the besieged garden, and especially the suffocation. There is something oppressive in a detailed picture of a swing hung by ropes from a wooden beam attached to posts, unmoving.

In fact, no movement, not even a light breeze, passes through this whole picture: neither the gate in the wall nor any door opens. No one enters and no one leaves. No dog barks, no bird flutters, no leaf trembles, everything is mute, everything is inanimate and congealed. Not a sound is heard in the entire passage. Not a murmur, not the movement of the softest breeze to shake the park, the garden, the plants, the weathervane rooster, the surface of the lake, the tethered boat, the frozen swing and the tops of the old plane trees. An inanimate world. The only movement in the entire description is, as we noted, the imperceptible advance of the shadow. And this spreads slowly: at first it falls on the flagstone path, from which it creeps toward the flower bed, and will eventually reach, twenty paces from there, the churchyard wall covered with tiny leaves of ivy. The interior of the house will remain sealed for several more pages. This is Effi Briest's world: the oppressiveness of the structures, the fossilized garden, the congealed lake. Only the creeping shadow cannot be stopped by walls.

What sort of contract does this opening passage demand from the reader as a prior condition to entering the house and the novel? A grave demand for slow and detailed reading: without extended observation one cannot discern the progress of the shadow. Without a patient ear, one cannot hear the totality of silence and congealment. Unless one internalizes the details, this opening paragraph is nothing more than a pleasant picture postcard of a grand noble home surrounded by a park and enveloped in tranquillity at the edge of a pond. The overeager reader may simply deduce that the rich are happy, and hurry on. The terms of Fontane's opening contract demand that we enter this novel on tiptoe, or almost. And that we take our time with what we are shown, that we listen silently to the gathering silence, even before we are introduced to Effi Briest herself.

Who Has Come?

On the Beginning of
"In the Prime of Her Life"
by S. Y. Agnon

Like *Effi Briest*, published about twenty-seven years earlier, *In the Prime of Her Life* is a story of a young woman married to an older man who had once been in love with her mother. Effi, in her day, agreed to the match with Instetten and had no expectation of love inasmuch as she had accepted and internalized the values of her social milieu to such an extent that in her view "surely he was the right man. Everyone is the right man. Of course, on condition that he is of the nobility and has standing and good looks." In contrast, Tirtza, the protagonist of "In the Prime of Her Life," very much wants to marry Akavia Mazal, struggles to have things her way, and is certain that Akavia is the right man according to her heart's desire and perhaps also according to a sort of intergenerational sense of justice. Unlike Effi, Tirtza does not accept what she takes to be the prevailing values in the world around her. For Tirtza, love takes precedence over everything: she loves Akavia Mazal—or perhaps she only loves the reflection of his image in her mother's unfulfilled love for him. She is even willing to become quite ill, using illness as an unconventional weapon to obtain the man she wants, even if he is not fervent about this match, or any other, and is not, in general, a fervent kind of person. Tirtza's aim is to correct an injustice that occurred in her parents' generation. At the end of the story the reader may realize—behind the narrator's back, as it were—that erotic injustice is irreparable. Incidentally, a small dog runs around from time to time in this story. It is not a mad dog, as in Agnon's novel *Just Yesterday;* in fact, it is rather friendly, but its name is Meu'vat, which means twisted, distorted, deformed.

In order to obtain what she wants, Tirtza makes her illness into a weapon, as if to say: If you do not give me Akavia, you will lose me the way you've lost my mother. The link between love and illness here is subtle and dialectical: Tirtza's mother was sickly and was therefore kept from Akavia, whereas Tirtza, by falling very ill, wins him. But Tirtza's love recalls the fire of Heraclitus: her victory is her defeat. Tirtza's married life is chilly, either because over the years the romantic idol had become a polite, considerate middle-aged gentleman or because this is what he always had been, outside mother's and daughter's romantic fantasies. To Tirtza, who tries to be her mother's identical twin, her husband begins to look like a twin of her own father (so much so that toward the end of the story she even mixes them up).

Tirtza's life with a man a generation older becomes an exact replica of her parents' marriage: gentle and considerate, but not what Tirtza had looked for. She sought not earth but the fire that had been withheld from her mother.

The motif of identical twins appears again and again in the story, filling it with confusions of identity both large and small, trivial and symbolic, comic and tragic. Every character seemingly embodies someone else. At the beginning of the story, even before we get to know who loves whom, several incidents of mistaken or misleading identity occur. But their significance will become known to the reader only at the end of the story. (Agnon himself once joked, in another context, that if a book is not worthy of being read twice one may as well not read it once.) The opening contract of "In the Prime of Her Life" demands, among other things, that the reader go back to the beginning after reading the whole story.

> In the prime of her life my mother died. She was about thirty years old at the time of her death. Short and bitter were the days of her life. All day long she sat in the house and did not leave it. Her friends and neighbors did not come to call and my father did not invite acquaintances either. Our house sat silent in its mourning, and its doors almost never opened to a stranger. My mother lay in her bed and spoke little. And when she spoke it was as if the wings of mercy had enfolded me and carried me to the Holy Sanctuary. How I loved her voice. Many times I would open the door so that she would ask who had come. I acted like a child. She would sometimes leave her bed and sit by the window. She would sit by the window in her white garments. Her garments were always white. Once my uncle David came to our city and saw

my mother and thought she was a nurse because her white clothes confused him and he did not know that she was the patient.

Her illness was a disease of the heart, which oppressed her. Each summer the doctors would send her to the healing springs, but almost as soon as she went she would return, saying that she had no respite from her longings. And again she would sit at the window or lie in her bed.

My father began to cut back on his business affairs. He did not even go to Germany, where he used to meet each year with his colleagues; my father was a grain merchant. This time he did not go. In those days, in that period, he neglected the ways of the world. And when he returned in the evening he would sit next to my mother. His left hand under his head and his right hand in hers. And she would sometimes take his hand to her lips and kiss it.

There are no fewer than three confusions of identity in these opening lines: Who has come and who has not come? Who is the patient and who is the nurse? And who are the lovers inspired by the Song of Songs?

Tirtza's relations with her mother are ritualistic. From the beginning of the story she sanctifies her mother, adores her ceremony of sitting by the window, worships her white garments. Later on she is overwhelmed by her mother's beauty, revels in her wonderful scent (although she wears no perfumes). The mystery surrounding the mother's delicate but stubborn manner of dying awakens in Tirtza a fierce excitement, which ultimately seals Tirtza's own fate. After her mother's death, she seeks to merge into the figure of her mother to the point of self-abnegation. Their ritualistic relationship prevents any real intimacy between mother and daughter, or maybe it is the other way around: lack of intimacy between mother and daughter evokes in Tirtza a worshipful attitude toward her mother. The mother has sunk into her illness and in the grief of her longings displays no desire for intimacy with Tirtza, nor even interest in her daughter's existence. She does not respond to the child's attempts to attract her attention.

Her mother's voice is, for Tirtza, like the song of angels: "When she spoke it was as if the wings of mercy had enfolded me and carried me to the Holy Sanctuary"; "How I loved her voice." But Tirtza's voice, almost the only sound she makes to her mother's ears, is the sound of the door, which opens "many times" (in a house where the "doors almost never opened to a stranger"). It is a childish, tantalizing sound: the mother is dying and the daughter plays a little prank on her. Just how cruel (but not malicious) this childish deception is, the reader will discover only later on, when it becomes clear that the sick woman who asks each time "Who is there?" might still be waiting for her loved man, come to bid her farewell. Again and again the mother learns that the opening of the door is no more than her daughter's childish prank, but, rather than chastise the child, she asks again who has come. As if to say: It is not for you that I wait.

Right from the beginning of the story Tirtza seems to be a neglected child. Her father is utterly engrossed in her mother; her mother is sunk in her love and in her farewell ceremonies; relatives and friends barely notice Tirtza. In contrast to the omniscient narrator in *Effi Briest*, Tirtza's view of her mother's final days is "esthetic" and emotional: she is beguiled by her mother's romantic fading away, by the white, melancholy halo that envelops the sick woman. Tirtza senses the "wings of mercy" transporting her to the "Holy Sanctuary." She is a one-person audience watching a one-woman show.

Even on the last day of her mother's life, Tirtza attempts to catch her mother's eye, if only for a moment: "The door opened three times and she did not ask who had come, and when I spoke to her she did not answer." The mother's last hours are spent in reading and burning letters, in long conference with her childhood friend Mintschi Gottlieb, and in a gentle but firm farewell to her husband. Not a moment, not a single word of explanation or of affection or farewell does she have for her only child, who struggles so hard to reach her through the code of the opening door. Not even a rebuke. ". . . and the words were written in script on thin paper, written in long and short lines. And when I saw my mother reading I said to myself that she would never neglect the writings." If Tirtza could distinguish the handwriting, the quality of the paper and the length of the lines, she had surely stood, at least for a moment, very close to her mother. Yet even at that moment the mother had not a word for her, not even a slight gesture of gentleness or attention.

As we have seen, the prank with the door was not the only confusion in the opening section of the story. An uncle who arrives for a visit mistakes the patient for a nurse because she is dressed in white. In the next paragraph the reader is misled to imagine that the father and the mother share a love inspired by the Song of Songs, "his left hand is under my head, and his right hand doth embrace me" (Song of Songs 2:6). In truth, the relationship between Tirtza's parents, one of gentle intimacy and melancholic solidarity, has not a whisper of the Song of Songs about it. In the scene before us, his left hand is not under her head and his right hand does not embrace her, but almost the opposite: "His left hand under his head and his right hand in hers." Instead of the Biblical embrace, there is only a holding of hands and, later, instead of the kiss there is only the kissing of a hand.

The mother's clothes, always white, strengthen the implicit identification of love and illness: the mother's dress is as white as a wedding gown, as a hospital gown, as a nurse's uniform, as shroud. The juxtaposition of weddings and death belongs indisputably to the repertoire of Romanticism: the lovers whose union has been prevented by societal or familial inhibitions are joined, despite everything, in their death (as, for example, in "Annabel Lee" by Edgar Allan Poe).

The beginning of "In the Prime of Her Life" is written as a carefully crafted parallelogram, so that even the horror is neatly balanced. Indeed the parallel lines and the Biblical Hebrew nuances in the story rely on a firm internal logic: both mother and daughter were students of Akavia Mazal, the Viennese intellectual and teacher who abandoned city life and went to live in a rented room on the edge of this small town, in a romantic "search for roots." He is a bit of a teacher, a bit of an Enlightenment poet, a bit of a historian who studies gravestones. Tirtza's father is concerned about her Hebrew education. Segal, the tutor, teaches her modern Hebrew. And Landa, the young man who courts her, writes letters to her in Biblical Hebrew.

Back to the opening lines of the story: the mother's life is fading away, and with it her husband's whole world. They are both so absorbed in their sorrow that they barely notice their daughter's existence. Nonetheless, the daily routine of an orderly, stable life are preserved throughout. This is somewhat reminiscent of the von Briest house in Hohen-Cremmen: a seemingly stable world with regular customs, good manners and habits of self-control. The Ming family has thrived for many years on the grain trade, on Jewish tradition, on the cycle of Holidays and on courtesy. There is a servant girl and there is—or could be—a nurse and a private tutor; there are regular trips to health spas abroad, and there are business trips to Germany.

In the opening of *Effi Briest* the immutable reality is shaped by a detailed description of the lines of the buildings, the walls and the garden, whereas here the stability of the family tradition is distinguished, first and foremost, in the writing style: a Biblical parallelogram presents us— from the very first lines of the story—with a world that stands, even in times of crisis and tragedy, on firm symmetrical pillars: "All day long she sat in the house and did not leave it" (literally: "All day long she sat in the house; out of the house she did not move").

There is, in the second lobe of this sentence, not a crumb of information not given to us in the first lobe. (A hasty style editor might have noted in the margin: Mr. Agnon, this is a superfluous repetition, should be deleted.) But the impact of such a sentence is created by the very fact that it has two equivalent lobes. A façade of stable balance, of equilibrium, of solid structures covers a social and familial reality whose internal equilibrium is increasingly shaken.

In the beginning of *Effi Briest* the creeping shade threatens the atmosphere of tranquillity, of affluence and of congealment that envelops the lordly house. So too, in the opening of "In the Prime of Her Life," the repressed love and impending death subvert the foundations of restraint and elegiac harmony offered by the style of the opening pages. The unfulfilled love undermines the pillars of a utilitarian marriage; repressed passions weaken the values of family and society; enlightenment—or perhaps only the sentimental echoes of enlightenment—subverts tradition; disaster underlies family harmony; and twinship and interchangeability threaten the very identity of the characters.

Were it not for Shakespeare's well-established claim to the title "A Comedy of Errors," we might use it for "In the Prime of Her Life," a story populated by doubles, a story about two women, mother and daughter, one married, loved and cherished by a man she docs not want, the other married to the man she wanted, only to discover later that he was not at all what she thought he was. It is a story of a husband who is, in effect, father and of a father who mirrors the husband. It is also the story of an infant who, seeing his father and his father's twin brother together, panics and bursts out in desperate, bewildered tears. It is also a tale of a brave young woman who, born into an era and a society that denied women the right of erotic choice, rebels—one of the first rebellious women in Hebrew literature; she breaks through the wall of tradition and gets what she wants. But she discovers that her victory is hollow, either because she has not figured out who she is and who the man is, and what are only mirror-images, or because she has become the victim of indirect radiation of a "sentimental education," full of "wings of mercy" and "holy sanctuaries" and illness draped with pure whiteness and death staged as a captivating marriage ceremony.

The opening lines set before the reader an entrapment of a contract.* The voice of Tirtza, the narrator, her cadenced Biblical language, her esthetic excitement at the elegiac-melancholy of her mother's illness and of her father's dedication, along with allusions to the Song of Songs, draw the reader into a veiled, emotional mood. They seem to prepare the ground for a story about heartbreak, orphanhood, love, the triumph of emotion over societal rules and class inhibitions. Yet if re-read, or if read backwards, *In the Prime of Her Life* reveals that Tirtza, having taken for herself what was denied her mother, might have been just a victim of a small intrigue perpetrated by a manipulative family friend.† In the end Tirtza is trapped in almost the same spot as her heartbroken mother. The reader is therefore directed, almost compelled, to return to the opening, to reexamine, as it were, the fine print of the contract. In doing so, the reader may establish that he has not at all been deceived: he might have been merely too hasty in trusting Tirtza's voice, not stopping to suspect her and her story, which is strewn from the very beginning with errors and with confused identities such as the prank with the door, which causes the mother repeatedly to ask, "Who is there?"

---

*Abraham Band, "The Undependable Narrator in *My Michael* and *In the Prime of Her Life,*" in the book *Shmuel Yosef Agnon, Selected Essays on His Work,* Hillel Barzel, editor; Am Oved Publishers, Tel Aviv, 1982, 320–329 (Hebrew).

†Nitza Ben Dov, *Agnon's Art of Indirection;* E. G. Brill, Leiden, New York, Koln, 1993, 107–133.

"Who is there?" rather than "Who is here?"

The mother's name is Leah. The Biblical story of Leah is also one of confused identities. Almost to the very last page of her recollections, Tirtza makes, as do other characters, errors of identity both large and small.

Leah's "soft" eyes, and her daughter Tirtza's eyes, and other eyes in this story are incessantly turned to "who is there." Perhaps because they are almost blind to who is here.

With an Expression of Very Respectable Importance

On the Beginning of Gogol's "The Nose"

The Nose" by Nikolai Gogol first appeared in 1836, sixty years before Fontane's *Effi Briest* and ninety years before Agnon's "In the Prime of Her Life." "The Nose" is the story of the nose of one Collegiate Assessor Kovalyov, a major by the name of Platon Kuzmich Kovalyov. This nose abandons its owner and sets off to wander around the city, dressed in an official uniform woven with gold threads, hires a carriage for its pleasure, piously bows and prays in church and is, in the end, arrested by the police when it is about to leave for Riga on an official passport. Major Kovalyov himself appears in the story much later than his nose. The opening scene takes place in the early-morning hours in the home of the barber Ivan Yakovlevich and his wife, Praskovya Osipovna, who are apparently a childless couple.

An extraordinarily strange thing happened in St Petersburg on 25 March. Ivan Yakovlevich, a barber

who lived on Voznesensky Avenue (his surname has
got lost and all that his shop-front signboard shows is
a gentleman with a lathered cheek and the inscription
'We also let blood'), woke up rather early one morning and smelt hot bread. As he sat up in bed he saw
his wife, who was a quite respectable lady and a great
coffee-drinker, taking some freshly baked rolls out of
the oven.

'I don't want any coffee today, Praskovya Osipovna,'
said Ivan Yakovlevich, 'I'll make do with some hot
rolls and onion instead.' (Here I must explain that
Ivan Yakovlevich would really have liked to have
had some coffee as well, but knew it was quite out
of the question to expect both coffee *and* rolls, since
Praskovya Osipovna did not take very kindly to these
whims of his.) 'Let the old fool have his bread, I
don't mind,' she thought. 'That means extra coffee
for me!' And she threw a roll on to the table.

Ivan pulled his frock-coat over his nightshirt for
decency's sake, sat down at the table, poured out
some salt, peeled two onions, took a knife and with a
determined expression on his face started cutting one
of the rolls.

When he had sliced the roll in two, he peered into
the middle and was amazed to see something white
there. Ivan carefully picked at it with his knife, and
felt it with his finger. 'Quite thick,' he said to himself.
'What on earth can it be?'

He poked two fingers in and pulled out—a nose!

He flopped back in his chair, and began rubbing
his eyes and feeling around in the roll again. Yes, it
was a nose all right, no mistake about that. And,
what's more, it seemed a very familiar nose. His face

filled with horror. But this horror was nothing compared with his wife's indignation.

'You beast, whose nose is *that* you've cut off?' she cried furiously. 'You scoundrel! You drunkard! I'll report it to the police myself, I will. You thief! Come to think of it, I've heard three customers say that when they come in for a shave you start pulling their noses about so much it's a wonder they stay on at all!'

But Ivan felt more dead than alive. He knew that the nose belonged to none other than Collegiate Assessor Kovalyov, whom he shaved on Wednesdays and Sundays.

'Wait a minute, Praskovya! I'll wrap it up in a piece of cloth and dump it in the corner. Let's leave it there for a bit, then I'll try and get rid of it.'

'I don't want to know! Do you think I'm going to let a sawn-off nose lie around in *my* room . . . you fathead! All you can do is strop that blasted razor of yours and let everything else go to pot. Layabout! Night-bird! And you expect me to cover up for you with the police! You filthy pig! Blockhead! Get that nose out of here, out! Do what you like with it, but I don't want that thing hanging around here a minute longer!'

In contrast to the opening sections of *Effi Briest* and *In the Prime of Her Life,* this is not a harmonious beginning, not even seemingly harmonious, but, rather, bureaucratic. The narrator's language, Gogol's language in his Petersburg stories, is meticulous and formal, illuminated sometimes by flashes of obsession and madness: he opens with a detailed report—including the month, the

day, the name of the city and the address of the house—
of "an extraordinarily strange thing." But even before he
gets to the event, his report strays off track, slips into
a pair of parentheses, and takes off on a chase after a
missing detail which is apparently crucial in order to
fill out the forms: the surname of the protagonist. The
chase after the name, which has been separated from its
owner and had "got lost"—as the nose will soon do—
drags the narrator from the home on Voznesensky Avenue to the barbershop, and from the barbershop to the
shop sign. Yet in the end he cannot find the missing detail
on the sign. But, compulsive reporter that he is, he takes
the trouble, while he is at it, to report the fact that on the
barbershop sign there is a picture of a gentleman with
lathered cheeks, a promise that "We also let blood," and
nothing more.

The narrator thereupon abandons the chase for the
surname, properly closes the parentheses, and continues
his story of the barber Ivan Yakovlevich with the words
"woke up rather early one morning and smelt hot bread."

What occurs in these first lines of the story, in the search
for the surname, will reoccur again and again throughout,
in the search for the lost nose. Anarchic forces lie in am-
bush for this story behind every bush, tempting it to
diverge from its path, attempting to dislodge it from the
proper, bureaucratic straight and narrow to which the
story presumably tries to stick, dragging it again and again
into shady side alleys.

The second attempt to make a proper start on the report—after the parenthetic bloodletting—begins with a
nose and the aroma of baking. This is not yet the cunning, arrogant nose of Major Kovalyov, not yet the story

of the birth of that nose from a freshly baked roll. At this point, we are invited to enter the story, with the aroma of the rolls baked by Praskovya Osipovna, via the drowsy nose of the barber whose surname has "got lost." The opening scene, until the cleaving of the nose, smells of a kind of tattered respectability, or of unwashed dignity, which will stubbornly present itself at unexpected moments throughout the story: when Ivan Yakovlevich sits up on his bed, he sees his spouse, "a quite respectable lady." (But how is "a quite respectable lady" different from just a "respectable lady"?) Later on he dons his "frock-coat over his nightshirt for decency's sake"(for whom? for what?), and before he breaks bread he assumes "a determined expression." From here until the end of the story, all of the characters will be more or less "quite respectable"; they will all make gestures of courtesy; they will all try to assume "a determined expression"; every one of them will flatter, cheat, fawn, fake or—conversely—patronize, swagger and humiliate the others. Major Kovalyov, for example, is not capable of any conversation with anyone other than condescending reproach or saccharine bootlicking. Even when he meets his own nose in church, his own "flesh and blood," which has abandoned him, he fawns before the arrogant nose because he does not dare to grasp it (the nose occupies a higher position than its owner and is dressed in a grander uniform). The tone of the story thus matches the quality of the reality it describes: a hierarchical reality, "quite respectable," draped in "a determined expression," tainted with bureaucratic stupidity and obsessive clerical detail accentuated here and there by flickers of madness; a reality in which all the characters look, at the same time, proper and hypocritical and decent and crooked ãnd overly well-mannered; a reality in which each one knows his exact place on the strict social ladder; each one torments his lessers and licks the boots of his betters. But throughout the story, a pack of anarchistic foxes incessantly nips at all the social conventions, insidiously ripping apart the societal mores, the prevailing order and the rules of logic.

Even before the barber (he, too, is described later in the story as a respectable man in a number of aspects) pulls the nose out of the roll, he performs a number of trivial actions which the hasty reader will not linger over since at a quick glance they amount to no more than a perfectly flat, pointless description of an ordinary boring breakfast; he peels onions, sprinkles salt and breaks bread. Careful observation, however, reveals that this routine takes place in reverse order, from the end to the beginning, so that the story is charged with little absurdities and nonsensical eccentricities even before the main absurdity of the walking nose occurs:

"Out of courtesy Ivan Yakovlevich put on a coat over his shirt, sat down at the table, poured out some salt, peeled two onions, took a knife. . . ."

But on what, in fact, did Ivan Yakovlevich pour the salt before he peeled the onions? And with what did he peel the onions before he took up a knife? Is our pedantic, bureaucratic narrator, who reports every detail so meticulously, really a negligent narrator? Perhaps an awful drunkard, like the barber and the Major, like most of his characters in this story?

Tiny distortions of logic like this, dreamy little mockeries, ghoulish grotesqueries, occur on almost every page. The opening of the work invites and prepares us to accept a skewered, deconstructed logic as an inseparable part of the forces at work here: deadening boredom, crude brutality, moral degeneracy and existential despair. Here, for example, is a short, fierce description which binds together boredom, contempt and distortion. Kovalyov returns home "on stumbling feet" from an unsuccessful chase after his lost nose.

It was already getting dark. After his fruitless inquiries his flat seemed extremely dismal and depressing. As he entered the hall he saw his footman Ivan lying on a soiled leather couch spitting at the ceiling, managing to hit the same spot with a fair degree of success. The nonchalance of the man infuriated him and Kovalyov hit him across the forehead with his hat and said: 'You fat pig! Haven't you anything better to do!'

Ivan promptly jumped up and rushed to take off Kovalyov's coat.

May the god of fools keep us from attaching an allegorical meaning to the nose as several critics have tried to do: the nose which gets up and goes out to wander in the city in the garb of a diplomatic adviser is not a parable for Tsarist-Russian society and does not represent the human condition. It is simply a nose, a walking nose with a little pimple on it.

True, Major Kovalyov is a regular philanderer, while our quite respectable lady, Praskovya Osipovna, is deeply contemptuous of her barber husband's virility, so that some readers are entitled to amuse themselves by speculating that Kovalyov's nose, which the husband pulls out one early morning from the depths of the lady's soft, warm roll, is actually meant to stand in for another organ; or one may even note that the discovery of a foreign object in the roll is described almost as the birth of an unexpected, unwanted offspring, a monstrous baby which arouses in the lady great anger and in her husband guilt and horror. (In the end, the poor barber cum "mid-wife" suggests wrapping it in a piece of cloth and getting rid of it, while the baker/mother hurries him with terrible rebukes: "Get that nose out of here, out! Do what you like with it, but I don't want that thing hanging around here a minute longer!"

The grotesquerie in the beginning of the story is expressed not just in the discovery of the nose in the roll. It also protrudes from the monstrous relations between the wretched husband and the wife who tyrannizes him with an iron fist. Every morning he must choose between coffee and bread because he is absolutely forbidden even to think out loud about asking for "both coffee *and* rolls, since Praskovya Osipovna did not take very kindly to these whims of his." When he chooses bread and forgoes coffee, Praskovya says to herself, "Let the old fool have his bread. . . . That means extra coffee for me!" When the nose is born out of the warm roll, Praskovya Osipovna, unlike her stunned husband, is not surprised but infuriated by the sight of the white thing that her husband "carefully picked at . . . with his knife, and felt . . . with his finger" before he pulled it out of the roll. The thin crust of etiquette, of respectability and of courtesy between husband and wife collapses, and reveals an abyss of terror and choleric hatred. One ought to take a brief look at the catalogue of invectives the barber's wife heaps upon her husband. Beast, drunkard, thief, fathead, layabout, filthy pig, blockhead. It is easy enough to discern that these invectives are not merely curses but also complaints, which reveal a bit of the relationship between the quite respectable lady and her husband, dressed, for decency's sake, in a frock-coat over his nightshirt before breakfast. Some of the insults are not necessarily directed at his professional incompetence as a barber who plucks off the noses of his customers, but sound more like coded complaints about the poor man's fading sexual resources.

The opening contract of "The Nose" is therefore a raggedy and dubious one. The narrator is at home in the musings of his characters yet does not know their surnames. He runs, as it were, right at the beginning of the story, from the home to the barbershop, chasing the surname on the shop sign, then returns full of superfluous information, but without the lost name. He also takes the trouble to present a façade of courtesy and mutual respect where, in fact, tyranny, miserliness, sexual frustration, and contempt reign.

From here on, throughout the story, this bureaucratic narrator will scurry from a pile of irritating details to a pile of self-righteous trivia, documenting it all with pedantic obsessiveness and narrow-mindedness, a seeming simpleton of a narrator forever defending his contemptible, greedy, arrogant, fawning, envious and deceitful characters, while leaving the reader to distinguish between wheat and chaff.

Yet even this is nothing more than a trap. Gogol's genius is expressed in, among other things, the fact that in the end it is his dishonest, irritating, obsessive narrator who is right. There is not and cannot be in this story any distinction between the wheat and the chaff. The trivia is the core. The raggedy, questionable opening contract is, after all, a fair one—because the world that Major Kovalyov's nose has set out to explore is itself raggedy, dubious, and deceitful.

A Log in a Freshet

*On the Beginning of Kafka's
"A Country Doctor"*

Kafka's story "A Country Doctor" (1919) is the tale of a country doctor who is summoned on a blustery, snowy night to the bedside of a seriously ill patient. The doctor answers the call, overcomes several strange obstacles, and manages to arrive at the patient's bedside, but is unable to help him. In the end he finds himself "with an earthly vehicle, unearthly horses, old man that I am, I wander astray." At the story's end the doctor says, "Betrayed! Betrayed! A false alarm on the night bell once answered—it cannot be made good, not ever." This closing sentence directs the reader back to the story's beginning, in order to investigate exactly where the doctor made the one and only mistake that can never be rectified. On the face of it, the story's end contains a certain moral. Seemingly, if the doctor had only known this moral early in the night, he would have been able to avoid the fatal mistake altogether.

But what in fact has the doctor, or the reader, learned by the end of the story? What was the mistake, and what is the moral? What is the "false alarm"? Could the doctor have chosen not to respond? Could he have known from the beginning that it was a false alarm? Is there a way (in this story, and perhaps beyond it) to distinguish between a false alarm and a true one? Ultimately, did the doctor indeed respond to the call or was he, after all, unwillingly catapulted on his way?

Actually, there is no alarm, no night bell at all in the beginning of the story—not a false alarm, or any kind of alarm. On the other hand, there is, at the beginning, a precise report of a factual, credible occurrence, in the course of which a nightmarish twist of events takes place. The reader will indeed have trouble locating a definite point at which this twist occurs. As in many of Kafka's works, there is no sudden change of gears, but, rather, a sort of intangible blurring of reality itself, a slippery, elusive distortion of dimensions, a metamorphosis through which everything is gradually suffused with the shades of a nightmare.

> I was in great perplexity; I had to start on an urgent journey; a seriously ill patient was waiting for me in a village ten miles off; a thick blizzard of snow filled all the wide spaces between him and me; I had a gig, a light gig with big wheels, exactly right for our country roads; muffled in furs, my bag of instruments in my hand, I was in the courtyard all ready for the journey; but there was no horse to be had, no horse. My own horse had died in the night, worn out by the fatigues of this icy winter; my servant girl was now running round the village trying to borrow a horse;

but it was hopeless, I knew it, and I stood there forlornly, with the snow gathering more and more thickly upon me, more and more unable to move. In the gateway the girl appeared, alone, and waved the lantern; of course, who would lend a horse at this time for such a journey? I strode through the courtyard once more; I could see no way out; in my confused distress I kicked at the dilapidated door of the yearlong uninhabited pigsty. It flew open and flapped to and fro on its hinges. A steam and smell as of horses came out from it. A dim stable lantern was swinging inside from a rope. A man, crouching on his hams in that low space, showed an open blue-eyed face. "Shall I yoke up?" he asked, crawling out on all fours. I did not know what to say and merely stooped down to see what else was in the sty. The servant girl was standing beside me. "You never know what you're going to find in your own house," she said, and we both laughed. "Hey there, Brother, hey there, Sister!" called the groom, and two horses, enormous creatures with powerful flanks, one after the other, their legs tucked close to their bodies, each well-shaped head lowered like a camel's, by sheer strength of buttocking squeezed out through the door hole which they filled entirely. But at once they were standing up, their legs long and their bodies steaming thickly. "Give him a hand," I said, and the willing girl hurried to help the groom with the harnessing. Yet hardly was she beside him when the groom clipped hold of her and pushed his face against hers. She screamed and fled back to me; on her cheek stood out in red the marks of two rows of teeth. "You brute," I yelled in fury, "do you want a whipping?" but in the same moment reflected that the man was a stranger; that I did not know where he came from, and that of his own free will he was helping me out when everyone else had failed me. As if he knew my thoughts he took no offense at my threat but, still busied with the horses, only turned round once towards me. "Get in," he said then, and indeed: everything was ready. A magnificent pair of horses, I observed, such as I had never sat behind, and I climbed in happily. "But I'll drive, you don't know the way," I said. "Of course," said he, "I'm not coming with you anyway," I'm staying with Rose." "No," shrieked Rose, fleeing into the house with a justified presentiment that her fate was inescapable; I heard the door chain rattle as she put it up; I heard the key turn in the lock; I could see, moreover, how she put out the lights in the entrance hall and in further flight all through the rooms to keep herself from being discovered. "You're coming with me," I said to the groom, "or I won't go, urgent as my journey is. I'm not thinking of paying for it by handing the girl over to you." "Gee up!" he said, clapped his hands; the gig whirled off like a log in a freshet; I could just hear the door of my house splitting and bursting as the groom charged at it and then I was deafened and blinded by a storming rush that steadily buffeted all my senses.

The story's title introduces us to the first-person narrator even before he says a single word: a country doctor. He then presents all the initial data in a matter-of-fact tone, almost like a police report; as though he was testifying before a jury, as though he must defend himself against criminal charges.

His condition: great perplexity. His problem: an urgent journey, a seriously ill patient, a village ten miles off, a blizzard, no horse and no hope of getting one. The measures he took: 1. Sent a servant to borrow a horse, despite the slim chance of success. 2. Stood in the yard, in the snow, ready and waiting for the journey, so that if the servant were to borrow a horse after all, not a minute would be lost. 3. Walked around the yard again. 4. Even kicked the door of the abandoned pigsty, in case he might find something there. 5. When the horses and the groom appeared, wasted no time in questioning the significance of their wondrous appearance. 6. Did not remain silent at the groom's attack on the girl, scolded him but did not tarry—getting to the seriously ill patient was still his highest priority. 7. Changed his priorities, when he realized that the groom was about to abuse Rose, and decided not to abandon her. 8. But when the groom made the horses dash forward, lost control over them and they galloped ahead dragging the wagon "like a log in a freshet."

The defense case appears solid and untainted. No jury could convict the doctor for his conduct at any stage of the events. Nevertheless, at the story's beginning and through to its end, the central questions remain unanswered. Moreover, they are never even asked.

Of what, exactly, is the doctor being accused? What allegation, what charge does he struggle so desperately to refute? Where do the accusations come from? Who convicts him? Who condemns him, in the end, to be "Naked, exposed to the frost of this most unhappy of ages, with an earthly vehicle, unearthly horses, old man that I am, I wander astray." And for what sin?

About one third of the story with the doctor's attempts to defend himself against an accusation that is never made, against a prosecutor who never once appears in this story. In addition to the logical and solid apology in the beginning of the story, another "defense plea" appears later, very different from the initial one, plaintive, awash in self-pity.

> I was the district doctor and did my duty to the uttermost, to the point where it became almost too much. I was badly paid and yet generous and helpful to the poor. . . . What was I doing there in that endless winter! My horse was dead, and not a single person in the village would lend me another. I had to get my team out of the pigsty; if they hadn't chanced to be horses I should have had to travel with swine. . . . I had once more been called out needlessly, I was used to that, the whole district made my life a torment with my night bell, but that I should have to sacrifice Rose this time as well . . . was too much to ask. . . .

In contrast to the defense brief in the beginning of the story, this monologue indicates, not an attempt to persuade, but an effort to arouse pity. Perhaps it is a monologue beyond despair, since the speaker has at the beginning expressed his desire to die (as soon as Rose is safe), and in the end he sums up his visit to the patient—and his whole life—as an irreparable failure.

Yet the opening of the story is, at least superficially, a solid, irreproachable defense. It is a dramatic defense: it is written almost as one long sentence, a multi-claused sentence whose parts are defined mainly by semicolons. The doctor's testimony is given in the present tense, like a live broadcast ("at the moment she went to him and here, yes, the groom grabs her and knocks his face against hers. The girl lets out a shriek and flees toward me"). There are several such mid-sentence transitions from past to present tense.

The doctor, who kicks the door open with his foot, delivers, to his astonishment, a groom and a pair of horses from the abandoned pigsty. Like the appearance of the nose from the roll in Gogol's story, the appearance of the groom and the horses in "A Country Doctor" is described almost as a birth: the groom crawled out "on all fours." And the horses "one after the other, their legs tucked close to their bodies . . . by sheer strength of buttocking squeezed out through the . . . hole which they filled entirely . . . their bodies steaming thickly." Biting Rose's cheek is the groom's first act, for which the doctor-narrator calls him a "brute." The groom's lust and his assault on the girl are indeed bestial. The doctor could hear the "door of my house splitting and bursting as the groom charged at it." At the same time, the groom fills the familiar role of the devil in a folk tale, proposing and delivering an unnatural deal, leaping from nowhere, offering to grant the customer something he desperately wants, but in return taking something far more meaningful. Here the doctor backs away from the deal at the last minute, turning it down ("I'm not thinking of paying for it by handing the girl over to you"), but the deal is forced upon him: once he agreed to use the devil's horses, he could not avoid paying the devil's price.

What appears at the beginning of the story as an effort to resolve a transportation problem—how can the doctor get to the bedside of his seriously ill patient on this snowy, stormy night—turns out to be an affair loaded with shame and guilt: the doctor's horse has died of overexertion, he was unable to protect the girl, and he also failed to cure the patient. Perhaps this is why the beginning—and, in fact, most of the story—is rendered as an apology. It is, however, an absurd, circular apology, almost reminiscent of the folk song. "There's a hole in my bucket": the first thing cannot be done for lack of the second, which is prevented by constraints of the third, which results from a shortage of the fourth, which can be filled only if the first thing is obtained. If we were to schematize the plot of "A Country Doctor" as a protocol of an interrogation, the absurdity of the doctor's condition, and of his defense, would become even more evident.

If everything is ready for the journey, including "a light gig with big wheels," why do you not go?

Because there is no horse.

Where is the horse?

Died last night.

And why did the horse die?

From "the fatigues of this icy winter."

And why was the horse fatigued in the icy winter?

Because "the whole district made my life a torment with my night bell."

And why was this call harder for you than others?

This time "I should have to sacrifice Rose."

And why did you abandon her? Why did you let the groom bite her face?

I reproached him. I threatened to whip him.

Why did you not whip him?

Because I immediately remembered "that the man was a stranger; that I did not know where he came from."

And why did you accept help from a stranger when you did not even know where he came from?

Because "of his own free will he was helping me out when everyone else failed me."

Why did the others fail you?

"The whole district made my life a torment."

And why did you not prevent him from breaking down the door and assaulting Rose?

I tried. I ordered him to go with me, and, if not, "I won't go, urgent as my journey is."

So why did you not cancel the journey?

Because the groom started the horses so sharply that the gig "whirled off like a log in a freshet."

But why did you put yourself into the hands of such a groom?

Because a seriously ill patient was waiting for me, and I did not have a horse.

And it's roundabout again. (Actually, the same format repeats itself later, in the episode of the misdiagnosis. The doctor first failed to notice the boy's injury, then failed to help him, paradoxically, there was no way he could. There was no malpractice or misconduct on the doctor's part. He is a good man who can do no good.)

What then is the "opening contract" the reader is asked to accept with the beginning of this story?

Initially, the reader is expected to trust the doctor-narrator, to feel sympathy for this decent fellow who responds to a seriously ill patient's call for help on a snowy, stormy night and who is delayed by a mere technicality; the reader must also acknowledge the sense of moral and professional obligation that binds doctors to do their utmost, even to endanger themselves if necessary, in order to provide medical assistance to seriously ill patients. The exigencies the doctor-narrator presents at the beginning of his "testimony" help to engage the reader in the necessity to focus on the main point (that is, saving the patient) and not to waste energy on anything else. A horse that died last night of cold and fatigue belongs to another story; there is no time for that right now, and anyway it won't help the horse. The groom and the pair of splendid horses suddenly born from an abandoned pigsty—well, they certainly arouse amazement, but one doesn't ask too many questions in a time of crisis. The reader is invited to identify with the sense of urgency that drives the doctor to decide to use those horses without asking questions.

Even the stranger's first abuse of the girl does not justify a postponement, and the reader is expected to be satisfied with the doctor's rebuke.

In short: until the horses break into a gallop, the reader has no reason to criticize the doctor's considerations. But when the situation spins out of the narrator's control, the reader is invited to ask himself whether the situation was ever under control in the first place. Were the doctor's decisions really decisions? What has been presented as an eminently reasonable chain of calculations and decisions was actually no more than a nightmarish hallucination: the doctor has been deceived. He has responded to the false alarm of the night bell, and nothing can "be made good, not ever." Not only has the doctor been misled, but the reader too, so it seems, has been taken for a ride.

Because in fact there was no alarm. Furthermore, did not the doctor choose to cancel the journey at the last minute, to reject the horse-for-wench deal, only to have his choice overridden by brute force? After all, he does not set out on his way, but is, rather, thrown into the journey against his will.

In utter contradiction to the impression made at the beginning of the story and reemphasized at its end, "A Country Doctor" is not a story of crime and punishment, nor is it a fable about taking the wrong turn or making the wrong choice: the doctor's tragedy is not at all a result of his actions or failures. The apologetics are superfluous. The opening contract is only the object of the real, the inner, conflict. According to the terms of this inner, latent contract, the doctor is guilty *a priori,* convicted and sentenced from the start, despite his innocence, even before he responds to the false alarm and even before he begins his series of apologies. From the very beginning, the doctor is no more than a "log in a freshet." He is found guilty only because a man's guilt is always lying in wait for him. Rose seems to set the terms of Kafka's contract as they really are when she says, "you never know what you're going to find in your own house." Guilt is always crouching behind "the dilapidated door of the year-long uninhabited pigsty."

Huge Losses

On the Beginning of Chekhov's "Rothschild's Fiddle"

The title of Chekhov's story "Rothschild's Fiddle," first published in 1894, misleads the reader on four counts: the Rothschild in the story is not the famed philanthropist; he is not a fiddler; the fiddle does not belong to him until near the end of the story; he is not even the protagonist but merely a supporting character, a poor wedding piper, an impoverished Jew.

The fiddle in the title actually belongs to one Yakov Ivanov, known to all as "Bronze." This Bronze, a Jew-hating old man, vulgar and heartless, earns his living as a coffin-maker and sometimes, for a few kopeks, plays his violin at weddings with a raggedy group of Jewish musicians.

Although "Rothschild's Fiddle" was published in the same year as *Effi Briest*, it does not depict a world of harmony, nor even a world of endangered harmony. One can, however, find a certain similarity between the begin-

48

ning of this story and the beginning of "A Country Doctor": the basic premise of the beginning, in both stories,
is disproved in the course of the story. The opening contract collapses eventually, revealing, in retrospect, a very
different type of contract: as in "A Country Doctor," here
in Chekhov's story the reader will have to reread and re-
assess everything.

Chekhov's world, suffused with subtle social observations, faint sorrow and compassionate humor, is, of
course, far removed from Kafka's nightmare world. But
the contract enfolded in the beginning of this story (and
in the beginning of several other Chekhov stories) is a
misleading one. Like the contract in "A Country Doctor,"
it is full of holes.

It was a small town, more miserable than a village,
inhabited almost exclusively by old men who died so
seldom it was very annoying. Moreover, very few
coffins were needed at the hospital and gaol. In short,
business was bad. If Yakov Ivanov had been a coffin-
maker in some large, provincial town he would most
likely have owned a house and been called 'Mr.
Ivanov.' But in this wretched dump he was simply
Yakov, his street nickname was Bronze for some reason and he lived wretchedly, like any common peasant, in a tiny old one-roomed cottage, which housed
himself, Marfa, a stove, a double bed, coffins, work-
bench and all his household goods.

. . . The local police inspector had been ill for two
years now and was wasting away. Yakov had impa-
tiently waited for him to die, but the inspector moved
to the main town in the district for treatment, and he
darned well gave up the ghost there. This meant a loss

of at least ten roubles, since the coffin would have been an expensive one lined with brocade. It was at night that Yakov was particularly plagued by thoughts of these losses. He would put his fiddle by his side on the bed and whenever he was haunted by any unpalatable thoughts, he would touch the strings, the fiddle would twang in the dark and he would feel better.

The tender sadness and the warm, forgiving humor might have left a stamp of sentimentality on "Rothschild's Fiddle" were they not balanced by an ice-cold selection of details, by a surgical conception of human nature and by a carefully measured distance between the characters and the truth. The characters are often unaware of this truth, or else they do not acknowledge it, but the reader is invited to recognize it between the lines. Here and in other stories, Chekhov establishes a precise equilibrium, as on a chemist's scale, between the ridiculous and the heartbreaking. The contract includes verbal understandings, as it were, between the narrator and the reader, a sort of non-paper consent, or secret appendix. Frequently the reader has to understand something by means of its opposite. Such, for instance, are the first sentences: a lamentation about the dearth of deaths in the village, about the old people who die "so seldom it was very annoying." This comes from the narrator, not from the protagonist, but the reader understands, after a moment of bewilderment, that the complaint is the grumbling of the coffin-maker, whose "business was bad."

Bronze and Marfa are an old, childless couple. The inventory of their humble hovel is counted by the narrator: "Marfa, a stove, a double bed, coffins, work-bench"— the woman, Marfa, is included in the list of furnishings—

but the reader already knows that this narrator mixes his own voice with the voice of heartless Bronze.

Bronze accepts, most reluctantly, orders for children's coffins, and calls the business of preparing such coffins "wasting my time on such nonsense." This detail, which appears near the beginning of the story, attests to petty avarice (small coffins make for small profits). Yet, halfway into the story, the reader will learn that Bronze has erased from his memory the life and death of his only child, a fair-haired baby girl born to Marfa and him fifty years before. Only after Marfa's death, when Bronze suddenly remembers his disaster, will it become clear to the reader that Bronze has hardened his heart all these years in order to protect himself from the pain. His aversion to making coffins for children was not just an expression of imbecilic greed, but also a hint of his hidden aversion to the death of children: the sad melodies that issue from Bronze's violin at night are but a stammering peasant version of *Kindertotenlieder*.

The opening contract is misleading because the narrator deliberately adopts the point of view of the old coffin-maker, as well as his language and his terms of reference, in doing so, the narrator obligates the reader to perform a task of cautious "translation": avarice is also a code word for deep loneliness. Contempt for constructing coffins for children camouflages the pain of bereavement. The revulsion aroused in Bronze by the whining melodies of Rothschild's flute is actually a defense against the reopening of wounds. The loathing he feels for Rothschild and all the Yids is mixed up with a clumsy, aggressive effort to suppress in himself a certain gut solidarity with the sufferers. As for the huge losses that Bronze laments, in the course of the story they assume proportions of lamentation for a wasted life and for the "vanity of vanities" of the human condition.

The plot is simple, even minimal: the tale of a village coffin-maker who ekes out a living, supplementing his income by playing his fiddle at weddings. He is miserly, grumpy and quarrelsome, with a heart hardened against both death and life: all his days appear to him as a continuous accumulation of financial losses. One day his wife becomes ill, and with silent joy accepts her impending death as a long-awaited release from the vale of tears. Seeing her joy, the coffin-maker feels regret for having treated her with unrelenting harshness. He drags the sick woman to the village doctor's and begs—as though bargaining—the doctor's helper, the only one there, to cure her. But the hard-hearted old man shrugs and soon turns to the next patient. The couple returns home, and the husband measures his wife and begins to make her coffin. He enters this "loss" in his ledger. In her final hours, his wife tries to remind him of their dead baby but he cannot remember. After her funeral, he himself feels ill, and, venting his violent wrath on the Jewish piper, who had come up to speak to him, wanders to the river, where the street boys yell at him. At home he remembers the baby and sums up his entire life as a series of deficits and losses. He wills his violin to Rothschild. After the coffin-maker's death, the Jew produces ineffably sad melodies from this violin.

The four "deceptions" in the story's title (Rothschild is not the baron; Rothschild is not a fiddler; Rothschild is not the protagonist of the story; the fiddle is not his) are unexpectedly put to rights at the end of the story: Rothschild is indeed made wealthy by his inheritance as he becomes the owner of the violin; he ceases to be a piper and becomes a fiddler, carrying on Bronze's melody. And so the reader first encounters the facts enfolded in the title, then discovers that they are all false, only to find out, at the very last moment, that they have been belatedly validated.

There is a subtle, elusive connection in this story between Jews and music, between music and soul. At first glance it seems that the story employs, through Bronze's perspective, a shopworn body of anti-Semitic clichés: the Yids are raucous, they smell of garlic, they are exploitative and greedy, whiny, cowardly, feeble, bootlicking. But the conclusion of the story turns everything upside down: the bequeathing of the violin and the transmigration of the melody turn Rothschild into the heir of the soulful person hidden behind the façade of a crude coffin-maker. "Rothschild's Fiddle" does indeed recall some of the flavor of Hassidic tales, as Bronze himself is reminiscent of the myth of the hidden just man.

The reader is asked to transform Bronze's recurring complaints about "losses" twice: a comic transformation and a tragic one. The comic transformation has to do with the fact that the tongue-tied Bronze always includes on the debit side of his ledger, not just real losses, but also unrealized income.

After all, it was a real river, not just a little stream. You could go fishing there, sell the fish to merchants, clerks and the buffet manager at the station, and then bank the proceeds. You could sail along it from one estate to another playing the fiddle, and all sorts of people would pay you. You could set up in the barge business again—that was better than coffin-making. Finally, you could raise geese, slaughter them and send them to Moscow in the winter. Probably the

down alone would bring in ten roubles a year. But
he had let the grass grow under his feet and done
none of this. The money he had lost! If you added
it all up—fishing, playing the fiddle, keeping barges,
slaughtering geese—what a packet he'd have made!

The tragic transformation contains Chekhov's great in-
novation, in both his stories and his plays: removing the
ancient barrier between comedy and tragedy; canceling
the strict convention that "low" characters, crude and ignorant types, necessarily belong to the comic realm—at
best they are sometimes thrown into pathetic distress—
while the tragic dimension is reserved exclusively for
the "noble." Only the noble, the enlightened, are able
"to take arms against a sea of troubles," to derive from
their suffering a comprehensive conclusion about fate, the
human condition, the existential absurd, or the hidden
flaw in their own character, because of which they were
doomed to fall.

Yakov Ivanov, alias Bronze, rises, at the point of his
death, to the heights of tragic awareness. Beyond his own
pointless life, in his clumsy and ignorant way, he thus
sketches the human condition:

> Life had passed without profit, without pleasure; it
> had gone by aimlessly, to no purpose. There was
> nothing to look forward to, and if you looked back,
> there was a terrible waste of money, enough to make
> your flesh creep. Why couldn't a man live without all
> that loss and waste? . . . he concluded that he stood
> only to profit by dying: he wouldn't have to eat,
> drink, pay taxes, insult people. Since a man lies in
> the grave not only for one year, but for hundreds and
> thousands, the profit would be enormous. . . . This

conclusion was correct, of course, but dreadfully unpalatable none the less. Why were things so strangely organized in this world, when you lived only once and had nothing to show for it?

This tragic monologue, which comes, not from the mouth of a hero or a philosopher-prince, but from the mouth of a greedy, narrow-minded, ignorant peasant, casts a totally different light on the opening of the story. The greed and vulgarity are not simply revealed as a thin outer shell, which the reader must remove in order to extract the pearl; greed, vulgarity and pearl are one. It is as if Chekhov cast the undertaker as the tragic Prince of Denmark. The tragic suffering, the tragic consciousness, and the protest against cosmic order come in this story right out of the depth.

Ultimately, where and how does Chekhov plant those unspoken understandings between writer and reader, behind the protagonist's back? We may hear them perhaps in the nocturnal melodies played by the coffin-maker when, trying to sleep in his solitary bed, he would reach for his fiddle. At such moments, Bronze becomes both a Saul tossed by evil spirits and a David, who "would touch the strings, the fiddle would twang in the dark and he would feel better."

The Heat and the Day
and the Wind

On the Beginning of S. Yizhar's Novel Mikdamot

The first section of S. Yizhar's novel *Mikdamot,* first published in 1992, is called "Gazing at a Place." Who *is* gazing? It is surmised—although not written—that the gazer is a person who wishes to return to the earliest experience etched in him. The effort to dredge up the deepest layers of memory, to reach the very bedrock, involves a paradox: one must put into words what has occurred long before one had words. What shimmers in the bottom of the writer's memory is not words but a string of sensations in which bursts the first flicker of the conscious I: ". . . who now saw and knew for the first time that here: he knows," or also: "had come to know the existence of all of this orange." The narrative consciousness, that which commands itself to recollect—like Nabakov's title *Speak, Memory*—is utterly dependent on words; yet it did not have words when for the first time it became aware of the world.

The opening contract therefore asks the reader to see through the words something that never was and never could be other than wordless.

And where was the first place? The very first? Because the first place, and without any proof, was the color orange. Wholly orange. Orange orange. Very orange. And completely.

Smooth as the smoothness of silk. And there was also a sort of careless flutter of curtains lush with orange. Orange unto deeply orange. And, it seems, there is no other logic, that these were no more than the lining of a very large tent, its insides rich with the rustle of very orange silk and an overflowing fecundity which moved in lazy waves all orange stirring soft waves. Illuminated orange and shaded orange, the orange in all variations of illumination, and in all the richness of its many responses, all utterly silky, in that great tent, in perhaps an army camp which was there, it seems (English? Turkish?), and not far from the place which Mother had come, it seems, and the baby in her arms (where is Father?) or had been invited perhaps to visit there, in the army encampment of tents, and this tent, the Indian tent (why Indian? But maybe Indian after all: an Indian tent in a British camp?), and this great tent, this billowing, which responds with lazy swells to the breath of the almost-absent wind, on that hot day, replying with a secretive murmur of silken orange to every touch of almost-wind, this silken orange so smooth and illumining and poured in to the knowledge of that observer, who now saw and knew for the first time that here: he knows, and to his very innards that here: now had

come to know the existence of all of this orange, all
the ripples of the orange silk, which skipped softly
and gently across the heights of this sensitive weave
which settled lightly, so full of orange splendor,
wholly orange splendor, here dull and here burnished,
chased by the almost-wind, inside a great tent, and
how could he have been there if not carried in his
mother's arms, at her bosom, at most two years
old? And cradled in her arms, held to her bosom, he
then suddenly discovered the vision of the thing, the
knowledge of this perfect orange, singular and general
and perfect and worldwide, flooding all with the sure
shine of orange, with a whispering breeze of smooth,
diaphanous silk, touchable and maybe even smellable,
on the lining of that very same Indian tent, slightly
limp, it seems, if indeed that is the true meaning of
the motion of that shimmering orange whole, and if
indeed all this is true, and if indeed he was really
there, then there was the place. And this was the place,
the primal first. And there was the beginning of everything, before all that came later, the beginning of the
heavens and the earth, the heat and the day and the
wind, and mother cradling in her arms, with the scent
of Mother, this was the first place.

The entire section seeks to appear outside time, like a
picture rather than a story, like one simultaneous sentence,
like a glance rebounding in the interior space of the tent,
spinning without progression in time. But the one long
sentence, measured in rhythmic phrases, incorporates a
second voice: again and again this voice slashes the first
one, investigating, doubting, verifying. The second voice is

almost always heard in parentheses and almost always presents questions: "English?" "Turkish?" "Where is Father?" "Why Indian?" "In a British camp?" "At most two years old?" "And if indeed all this is true, and if indeed he was really there."

The first, the main voice, struggles to touch the naked senses: Whispering, smooth, touchable, smellable, limp, motion. Whereas the second voice restricts, identifies, locates and defines, the first voice is primeval; the second, as though seeking to restrain the first, is interrogating, demanding proof: "And how could he have been there if not carried in his mother's arms, at her bosom?" The first is a synesthetic one, uniting disparate senses ("whispering breeze of smooth, diaphanous silk, touchable and maybe even smellable"). At the conclusion of the section, as if the rising tension between the two contradicting voices reaches some sort of resolution, the first voice recalls "mother cradling in her arms, with the scent of Mother," and the second voice lays aside its skepticism and confirms, in one short pronouncement, everything that has been painted in the very long sentence: "this was the first place."

Yet the orange Indian tent is not the first place, but perhaps a reflection of the first place. The Indian tent is merely the first place in which the narrator "suddenly discovered the vision of the thing." Underneath this discovery there apparently flickers something earlier than this: mother's womb. "Smooth as the smoothness of silk . . . flutter of curtains lush with orange . . . were no more than the lining of a very large tent, its insides rich with . . . overflowing fecundity . . . all utterly silky . . . and there was the beginning of everything . . . the beginning of the heavens and the earth, the heat and the day and the wind, and mother cradling in her arms, with the scent of Mother. . . ."

The person gazing at the place is actually gazing simultaneously at two places, which have been imprinted upon each other: the womb and the tent, the first string of sensations and the first moment of recognition. The moment those two revelations are combined, the "I" begins to be I. (Immanuel Kant found that unconscious sensations are "blind," whereas insensate consciousness is "empty.")

The language itself is, by its very nature, an obstacle to the attempt to describe the birth of the "I." The words must come one *after* the other, while the wealth of sensations of the orange are taking place one *within* another. The narrator therefore tries to break free of language's handcuffs, to shape with words something in which words have no part. To that end he separates the word "place" from its usual meaning: throughout the first section of *Mikdamot* the reader is invited to substitute "moment" for "place": "And there was the beginning of everything . . . this was the first place." (By the way, there are several Hebrew expressions in which concepts of place indicate time, and vice versa, as in English: "from here on in," "beforehand," "the top of the hour," "high noon."

The book's opening section demands that the reader take part in eliminating the barrier between place and time. "Place," on this page, is not a location, but a plethora of awakenings of the "I" to the abundant glimmerings of the world. In any event, so claims the first voice.

"Because the first place . . . was the color orange."

"Orange" appears no fewer than twenty-three times on the opening page of *Mikdamot*. Furthermore, there are twenty-two words in the opening sentence of the Hebrew text, among them five are "orange" and four are "first," and there is also "wholly," "very," "completely." A mantic act, an act of conjuring up memory by sorcery, lies in these repetitions: first orange orange first orange first. The hue of sun and oranges is therefore the overt hue of the word in the narrator's memory, and it will be the predominant hue of most of *Mikdamot*.

In contrast to the opening contract in many stories, this opening contract does not offer the reader an account of what happened to whom, when and where. There is no "exposition" in the usual sense, a kind of information desk placed by the main entrance of the story, providing the reader with the necessary information for the journey. True, the second voice repeatedly interrogates the first one from within pairs of parentheses—Was the army camp English? Or Turkish? Was the tent Indian? And where was Father?—as if repeatedly calling the first one to order, demanding that it fulfill its "expositional duty."

Mantic invocation such as "first orange first orange first," repetition of a phrase or a sound or an image that is meant to conjure the cave of memory so that it will yield some treasure buried deep beneath the sandy bed of forgetfulness—all are rather common in literature. Many stories describe the initial encounter between "I" and "it," the crystallization of the "I" through the first recognition of the "not I." One is reminded, for instance, of the moocow, the wild rose blossoms and the song of the eye-gouging eagles in the opening of Joyce's *Portrait of the Artist as a Young Man;* thus the detailed recollections in the twilight zone between sleep and wakefulness and the *petites madeleines,* prompt Proust's memory to set out in search of *Remembrance of Things Past;* and thus, too, functions the hypnotic repetitive mantra in the opening of Thomas Wolfe's *Look Homeward, Angel:* "... a stone, a leaf, an unfound door ... Where? When?"

In the opening contract of *Mikdamot,* the reader is requested to retreat all the way to the synesthetic, multisensory experience, to the perception of being as it was before the separation of the senses and before the division of labor among the senses: the reader must take it upon himself to sail, from the very first sentence, into a world where place is color, the (sole) color is orange, and the orange is silken soft, and rustling, and moves in lazy waves and is both illuminated and shaded at turns, and is also capable of "changing responses," and turns to "orange dust," and this orange dust "is blown silently, secretly," but also shines, whispers, and is "diaphanous, touchable and maybe even smellable." (Incidentally, there is a similar attempt to reach out and touch experience before the differentiation of the senses in several poems by Chaim Nachman Bialik: in *Zephrys,* in *Zohar,* in *The Pool,* and in his story "Aftergrowth.")

A reader who is unable or unwilling to go with the mystical elimination of the barriers between the senses and between feelings, between the sense and the sensed, will miss *Mikdamot* altogether. At best, such a reader might just cross it holding tight to the "guardrail" which the "second voice" provides; he will come out the other side of this text with no more than an informative envelope as flimsy as an eggshell: the story of someone who verbosely recounts how, as a babe in his mother's arms, he visited some tent, maybe an Indian tent, in some army camp, maybe a British or Turkish camp, wrapped in a cloud of verbal orange fog.

Yet all this in this opening section is not a fog, but a paradoxical use of language to reach what is beyond language; to reach what had been before words; to reach what is contradictory to the very confining, fixative nature of words: language is, after all, a tool we use mostly to mark, to define, to clarify, to separate and distinguish. In the opening section of *Mikdamot,* however, language seeks to reunify the world and return it to its primeval, pan-sensual essence. The words, by their nature, must come in a sequential line, one after another, thus imposing a linear, chronological determinism on everything. In the opening, the words do not arrange themselves in a line and do not delineate a line: they spread rather like ripples. The eye of these ripples, the pebbles that create shimmering circles in this text, are the words "place," "orange," "first."

How can one reach with words the primordial experience that words, by their very presence, undermine?

By breaking the rules, for instance: the Indian tent - "responds with lazy swells" to the breath of the no-windiness. (I once heard a woman, an immigrant from Hungary, coining a similar idiom: complaining about the fact that there was no water from the faucet, she said: "There is no waterlessness.")

Or by crafting the entire opening section as one continuous sentence that (ideally) has no earlier and no later.

Or by using parentheses to create a fugue between the first and second voices.

Or by epiphanic flickers: ". . . he then suddenly discovered the vision of the thing, the knowledge of this perfect orange, singular and general and perfect and worldwide, flooding all. . . ."

But mainly by the use of words as tones, rather than as markers, in clusters of onomatopoeia, in medleys of melodic variations, so that language suddenly ceases to denote, ceases to inform, and begins to sing and dance:

> The first place the first the first
> The first place without any proof
> Was the color orange wholly orange
> Orange orange very orange

Or thus:

> And there was the beginning of all,
> Before everything that came later
> The beginning of heavens and earth
> And heat and the day and the wind.

Into Mother's Bosom

On Several Beginnings in Elsa Morante's History: A Novel

In 1994, Elsa Morante's great novel *La Storia* (1974) appeared in Hebrew translation by the late Emmanuel Beeri; it had appeared in English as *History: A Novel* in 1977. It is the story of an epileptic teacher, Ida Mancuso, née Ramundo, her son Antonio (Nino, also known as Ninnuzza and Ninnarieddu) and her younger son Giuseppe, called Useppe, born during the Second World War after a German soldier named Gunther raped her twice, less than three days before he was killed on his way to the battlefront in Africa. On top of this, *La Storia* takes upon itself the task of summarizing and condemning, in several pages at the beginning of each chapter, half a century of world history.

Ida's attitude toward the world is sharply defined as an attitude "of frightened awe." This awe is mixed with "passive sweetness of a very profound and incurable barbarism," which brings to mind "the mysterious idiocy of animals, who, not with their mind, but with a sense in their vulnerable bodies, 'know' . . . the *sense of the sacred.*" Such a mystical sense, such a bestial-holy idiocy and frightened awe of "the world" can also be found in the Jesus-like character of the child Useppe, and perhaps even in his German progenitor, Gunther, the childish, heartbreaking rapist.

The "contract" in the opening of *La Storia* invites the reader to take a stand on the correct side of the political barricades separating the children of light from the children of darkness: on one side, history, full of war-mongering dictators, bloodsucking capitalists, scheming politicians,* and, on the other side, there is the essence of purity and light: the young woman bringing forth a son, and both, young woman and son, are pure and holy. Mother and child are circled by a group of meek, mild secondary characters: the saintly prostitute, the tormented Jew, the pure-hearted working-class neighbors, simple folk, mute souls, all of them good and gentle but crushed under the wheels of history. At first glance, this is nothing more than a proletarian folk allegory in black and white, with a strong whiff of anarchist or proto-communist ideas, nostalgic for the catacumbal ordeal of the early Christians.

In the front of the book are two epigraphs:

"There is no word in the human language capable of consoling the guinea pigs who do not know the reason for their death." —A survivor of Hiroshima

---

* "History is a sequence of robberies in broad daylight / crime, retribution and more crime / are just stupidity and betrayal apart" (N. Alterman, *Poems of the Plagues*).

". . . Thou hast hid these things from the wise and prudent, and hast revealed them unto babes . . . for so it seemed good in thy sight." —Luke 10:21

Can these quotations be seen as an opening contract? Or a preliminary commitment prior to the signing of the contract?

The first quote reflects the moral position of the novel regarding the Second World War: according to the chronicler in *La Storia,* this was not a war of the Allies against a Nazi-Fascist coalition; rather, it was an assault by governments, all of them despicable, against the simple man, the "guinea pig." The second quote expresses a Christian sentiment: the babes are close to God, the wise are distant from Him.

The first section of *La Storia* opens with several pages of "popular" chronicle, a summary of the political, economic and social events of the first forty years of the twentieth century, pictured as a never-ending struggle between the good oppressed masses and a handful of wicked, manipulative masters.

The reader is therefore required to decide "up front" whether he is willing, as a precondition of entrance to the work, to don a sort of ideological straitjacket (which the novel actually manages to shed several pages later, only to put it on again from time to time, particularly in the pages of chronicle between chapters). Some of these are:

1900–1905
  The latest scientific discoveries concerning the structure of matter mark the beginning of the atomic century.

1906–1913

Nothing very new, in the great world. Like all the centuries and the millennia that have preceded it on earth, the new century also observes the well-known immoble principle of historical dynamics: power to some, servitude to the others. And on this rule are based, in agreement, both the internal order of society (at present dominated by the "Powerful," known as the capitalists) and the international order (known as imperialism) dominated by certain Nations also known as "Powers," which have virtually divided the entire surface of the globe into their respective properties, or Empires. Among them, the latest arrival is Italy, which aspires to the rank of Great Power. . . .

1915–1917

. . . In Russia, end of the war against the great Powers, following the Marxist revolution for international social-communism . . .

1919–1920

Absent from the peace table is Russia, now surrounded and reduced to an international battlefield. . . . In this crucial test, and amid massacres, epidemics, and poverty, the Comintern (the Communist International) is founded in Moscow. It summons all the world's proletariat . . . to the common goal of revolutionary unity, striving towards the International Republic of the proletariat.

1922

After years of civil war in Russia, ending with the victory of the revolutionaries, the new state, the USSR, has been formed. It is to represent the symbol of hope for all the "wretched of the earth." . . .

And so on and so forth, until the reader finds it difficult to decide if this is a rough draft written by an old-time propagandist commissar before addressing the masses, or maybe it is just a parody of such a draft. This Manichean manifesto reappears at the beginning of each section of the novel. Such political intermezzos counterpoint the life of Ida and her children. This stuff captures the concluding pages of the novel, which denounce the "progressive and colossal development of history . . . devouring the best energies. . . . Instead of serving man, machines enslave him. . . . The proliferation of arms is accompanied by the proliferation of ridiculous consumer goods. . . . Artificial products (plastic) alien to the biological cycle transform land and sea into a deposit of indestructible refuse . . . the industrial cancer spreads . . . popular media . . . are used to . . . propagandize an inferior 'culture.' "

And there are various and sundry bits from the jargon of the old left, mixed with a touch of "flower children" flavor, spiced here and here with an ecological sigh. Morante seems to make use of the whole spectrum of arguments and slogans of those who despise the twentieth century, from left and right, without distinction. It is as though she has taken upon herself the job of demonstrating just how similar progressive jargon and reactionary jargon can sometimes be.

The notion of the unending struggle between "crushing history" and "the sacredness of daily life," just like the dream of the triumph of the pure-hearted "little guy" over the rotten "establishment," has fascinated many artists, perhaps from the time when Cervantes made Sancho Panza the carefree popular ruler of Barataria Island (which was not even an island), to the time of Bertolt Brecht and Charlie Chaplin.

On the next-to-last text page the "sermon" is cut off: ". . . . . and History continues . . . . ." This is as abrupt as the new leaf turned at the beginning:

> One January afternoon in the year 1941, a German soldier was out walking . . . through the San Lorenzo district of Rome. It was about two o'clock in the afternoon. . . .

The soldier is not touring the archeological or architectural treasures of Rome. He is hoping to find a brothel: that very night he will be sent with his unit to the battlefront.

And with this, a new contract seemingly unconnected to the introductory quotations, very distant from the opening manifesto, is offered to the reader. If the first contract invited the reader to accept a simplistic axiom ("The little people are very nice but the rich and the powerful always exploit them and oppress them with wars"), from here on the rich and powerful no longer appear on the story's stage. Crimes from now on take place between the good guys and the good guys: the rapist and his victim in the latter part of the first chapter, both of them members of the camp of the enslaved little people. In resounding contrast to the banner hanging across the entry gate of the novel, evil will be revealed here as an apolitical, ahistoric force, which flows perhaps from the very same springs as childlike purity. The Manichean placard dissolves into a subtle and compelling picture of the birth of evil and savagery out of the spirit of innocence. That which had begun as a description of the bitter battle between "history" (that is, the injustices caused by the powerful and the wealthy) and "life" (that is, the apotheosis of the daily existence of the little survivors) does not end here in a red revolution, but instead becomes a realistic poetic novel, bordering on a mystical passion.

This is how Gunther, the young German soldier, is described:

> . . . in contrast with his martial stride, he had a desperate expression in his eyes. His face betrayed an incredible immaturity, although he was six feet tall, more or less. And the uniform . . . was short at the waist and in the sleeves, exposing his thick wrists . . . like a worker's or peasant's. . . . And until the time of his summons to his military duties, he had always lived with his brothers and his widowed mother in his native home in Bavaria, near Munich . . . where he went to do some jobs as an electrician and where, rather recently, he had learned to make love, thanks to an elderly prostitute.

The village boy who had never gone farther than Munich feels, of course, elated by the uniform in which he has been dressed, by the chance of a hasty lay in Rome, by "superheroic acts, in honor of his Führer," and, especially, by the rumor of the imminent transfer of his unit to Africa:

> . . . he was impatient for adventure; but to some extent, also, unknown to himself, he remained a mamma's boy. . . . At other times . . . he brooded constantly, in bitter compassion, about his prostitute in Munich, thinking how she wouldn't find many customers these days, because she was old.

But several minutes later this mamma's boy, this compassionate lad, with "worker's or peasant's" wrists, enters a smoky cellar, "Remo's—Wine and Food," orders some wine (just to show off, because in fact he prefers beer), and for the sake of showing off he even downs the wine "in great gulps, like a Sardinian bandit," and then, suddenly,

> violently flung on the counter almost all the scant money he had in his pocket; while his anger tempted him to knock over the counter and the tables and to behave not like an ally but like an invader and a murderer. However, a slight nausea was rising from his stomach, and it dissuaded him from any action.

The "slight nausea" will not stop him a little later when he rapes the woman (who could have been his mother): one can see the branching of violence and evil from the very root of innocence and "bitter compassion" for the first time—but not the last time—in this amazing novel. Gunther goes into a violent fit of fury only because it seems to him that the waiter and the restaurant owner like him a little less than he deserves, and do not go out of their way to quench his gnawing thirst for love: "There is just not enough love to go round. . . ."

This thirst for love, the repressed longing for mother's apron strings, leads Gunther, after leaving Remo's, to "stop at random at a doorway, with the carefree notion of huddling up in there and sleeping, perhaps on a step or in the area beneath the stairs. . . ." Neither carnal lust nor an itch for violence, but, rather, the "notion of . . . sleeping" perpetrates what follows.

> . . . The first female creature who happened to come in that doorway (we don't mean just an ordinary girl or some little neighborhood whore, but any female animal: a mare, a cow, a she-ass!), if she looked at

him with a barely human eye—he would have been capable of embracing her violently, or perhaps flinging himself at her feet like a lover, calling her: meine Mutter!

Almost instantly his innocent prayer is answered, and a "female creature" appears: Ida Ramundo, the widow of Mancuso, returns home, burdened with bundles and shopping bags.

And thus in a novel whose opening contract has insisted that the reader recognize all of the world's evil as caused by the establishment in its various guises, and that the fount of grace and mercy is children, peasants, laborers, women, the simple folk, the plot actually results from a brutal act of rape committed by an innocent child, a simple fellow. It was precisely this "child's" guileless thirst to curl up at his mother's bosom—a desire which Christianity has always invested with the symbolic glow of sanctity—which led to a burst of raging violence.

What then has *La Storia* shown us about the birth of evil in the very heart of proletarian and common folk, and good-Christian purity? About the birth of savagery out of thirst for love? Have we again been shown Hannah Arendt's dusty wisdom about the "banality of evil"? Or has a different landscape been revealed here, a horrifying landscape illumined by Elsa Morante with nightmarish light, like a Hieronymus Bosch painting (a nightmarish light mixed with nausea, terror and mercy), far from the self-righteous didactic-socialistic light she herself set for us in the entry hall of this strange novel?

With this said and done, we are expected to ignore the opening contract as manifested in the introductory quotations. We are even requested to wave good-by to the "chronicle" in the beginning of the book, and to depart from the realistic-psychological convention in the description of Gunther's origins and Ida's background. We must examine the new "contract" contained in the rape scene, the point at which—at least fifty pages after the book has begun—the plot at last opens and begins to evolve.

The horrors of history and the cruelty of establishments may well be the remote cause for the characters' suffering, but the root of evil is not "external," it is not in the fat cigar-smoking capitalists and their fascist warmongering lackeys. A deep, ahistorical level of evil is revealed in the scene of the rape. It is a scene with only two characters in the room, a man and a woman, both of them good and simple souls. But one good soul suddenly inflicts pain and humiliation on the other good soul. How can this be? From where has evil sprung?

We must examine this scene carefully. It begins when the soldier notices a woman returning to her home and shouts to her one of the four words he knows in Italian: "Signorina! Signorina!" then suddenly, instantaneously, and "with a leap he appeared before her although he himself didn't know what to demand."

And why with a "leap"? And what does he want from her? The woman, on the other hand, "stared at him with an absolutely inhuman gaze, as if confronted by the true and recognizable face of horror."

But why? What is it in him, in this lively young man, which turns him—in her eyes—into the "recognizable face of horror"?

On the surface it seems that the reader is then given a many-page answer to this question (the story of Ida's life up to the day of the rape). The essence of the answer is that Ida Ramundo Mancuso was born and raised in the shadow of family secrets that have given her a deathly fear of authority: her father was a covert anarchist; her mother, a secret Jew; Ida herself, a closet epileptic and half-Jew. It is actually not the boy who is the "recognizable face of horror" in Ida's eyes but his uniform. Had her secrets been revealed? Had the authorities finally exposed her?

> He must be an agent of the "Racial Committee" . . . come to identify her. For her, he had no features of his own. He was a copy of the thousands of similar faces that multiplied to infinity the sole, incomprehensible face of her persecution.
>
> The soldier was offended, feeling the unknown lady's evident and extraordinary disgust was an injustice. He wasn't accustomed to inspiring disgust in women. . . . However, in his mortification, instead of giving up, he insisted. When the family cat . . . crouches in his private hiding-places, the children persist in hunting him.

So the good woman was startled (for entirely understandable reasons), and the good boy was insulted by her fright (for reasons that are also entirely understandable). On the face of it, it would seem that they could clear up the misunderstanding, dissipate the fright (which was, after all, unfounded: the soldier did not come to arrest her) and easily undo the insult (she did not mean to insult him).

It is worth noting that the woman arouses in the rapist—moments before the rape—neither sexual desire nor an urge to violence. The woman's fright has in it no trace of fear of rape, only fear of arrest: the rape is not "hanging in the air"; the tension between them is not at all male-female; she fears him, he is hurt by her fearing him, and that's all there is to it just a couple of minutes before the rape.

From where then have "hunting" and "family cat" appeared?

Well, once the helpless other is totally at your mercy, this other becomes a frightened family cat. As though without noticing, having done nothing, with no intention of frightening, you have suddenly scared her terribly; you are strong; you are in control; you are the hunter.

The very same "signal," whose content is "I am entirely in your hands, helpless, at your mercy," can arouse in its recipient either mercy or brutality, either compassion or domination, either gentleness or sadism.

The rivulets of mercy and the current of evil flow from the same source: and this, it seems, is the theological observation that flickers, in a complex and subtle manner, over the rape scene. This observation is very far removed from the social-political credo presented at the beginning of the novel.

For that matter, she didn't even try to move aside. Her only act was to hide in one of her shopping bags . . . some school copybook she was holding. . . . She saw herself, stripped now of every disguise, down to her private, half-Jewish heart, there before him.

The copybook is incriminating evidence, because according to the racial laws she is forbidden, as a half-Jew, to be a teacher. There is, it appears, no sexual aspect to her terrified "nakedness": this is the nakedness of a bird fluttering in the hunter's hand. But it is precisely this kind of nakedness, this helplessness, this birdlike flutter, that

arouses in the boy a kind of convulsive "masculinity."
The subtlety of the following description shapes with surgical precision the watershed, the microscopic turning
point between a gentlemanly code of chivalry and the
mode of the hunter-rapist.

> Resolutely, on a gallant-bandit impulse, he took the
> bundles and shopping bags from her hands; and with
> a trapeze-artist's leap, he preceded her forthwith up
> the stairs. At each landing, he stopped to wait for her,
> like a son who, coming home with his slow mother,
> acts as scout. And she followed him, stumbling at
> every step, like a petty thief dragging himself behind
> the bearers of his cross. . . . On the sixth landing, they
> had arrived. And when, bathed in icy sweat, she had
> trouble dealing with the lock, the German put the
> bags on the floor and promptly lent her a hand, like
> someone coming into his own home.

And the "gallant-bandit impulse" is a reoccurrence of
the "masculine" show-off at the restaurant, when Gunther (even though he really preferred beer) ordered a glass
of wine and drank it in "great gulps, like a Sardinian bandit." There, in the restaurant, after he is not received with
the love he needs, he turns right away into a "bandit," is
filled with a furious urge to upend the counter and the
tables, to act like "an invader and a murderer." Here then
is the anatomy of the tunnel that leads from love, gentleness and mercy to gallantry, to masculinity and finally to
savagery: the child asks to be loved and is rejected, therefore throws his money on the counter, causing terror and
enjoying it. By virtue of the other's weakness and panic
the child swells into a warrior, dressed in a hackneyed

77

combination of masculine images, "gallant bandit," and the next thing you know he becomes "an invader and a murderer."

As for Ida, she is headed for disaster—not as an innocent lamb in the hands of her shearers, but feeling she is a sinner deserving of punishment, "like a petty thief dragging himself behind the bearers of his cross." This is a clear Christian image, which makes Ida Ramundo reminiscent not of Christ but precisely of the two thieves who were crucified to his right and left, or, rather, of one of them, the "good thief," to whom Jesus makes his promise, from the cross, that "Today shalt thou be with me in paradise" (Luke 23:43).

She feels like "a petty thief" not just at the sight of the Nazi uniform, but always: ever since the days of her childhood, she has felt she is a sinner, always, to everyone. Her mother before her also lived her life with humiliation and submissiveness, "like a petty thief," because of the shameful secrets that were constantly in danger of being exposed (Jewishness, anarchism, epilepsy).

The shame and the fear blind Ida so that she is unable to discern what she could have seen from the first moment, were she only able to glance back at the boy behind the uniform: this Nazi does not stand before her in the name of law and authority, but as an abashed beggar who reaches for a handout of a little motherly love. (The good Ida would almost certainly have granted Gunther some warmth, a few scraps of motherly affection, were her eyes not blinded by her panic.)

Gunther's eyes, on the other hand, are unable to see that the "insult" to him is not due to rejection of his plea but to terror inspired by his uniform, and that he himself, the mighty and fear-inflicting "gallant bandit," needs attention, gentleness and a soothing caress even more than he craves a quick lay. The blindness of Ida, the "petty thief," turns her into a persecuted animal, "bathed in icy sweat," "stripped now of every disguise." And now the persecuted animal, who had formerly "mistreated" him and is now startled and "stripped," generates in Gunther, like a chain reaction, the feeling of "a son . . . coming home with his . . . mother," which changes to a feeling of being a "gallant bandit," then swells to a feeling of "masculinity" and "savagery," and finally becomes the thrill of the hunter at the submission of his hypnotized prey.

The interior consisted of two rooms in all, plus lavatory and kitchen; and it displayed, besides its untidiness, the coupled desolation of poverty and the lower middle class. But the immediate effect of that place on the young soldier was a savage homesickness and melancholy, because of some slight affinities with his maternal house in Bavaria. His desire to play vanished like the smoke of a Bengal light; and his drunkenness, not yet worn off, became a feverish bitterness in his body. Plunging into total silence; he began to march among the considerable clutter of the room with the tough look of a stray starving wolf, seeking something to appease his hunger in an alien lair.

In Ida's eyes, this look corresponded exactly to his police duties. Preparing herself for a general search, she remembered the paper with Nino's family tree . . . among other important documents; and she wondered if those enigmatic marks would not be obvious clues for him.

And so this tragedy of errors evolves. The meek lamb terrifies Ida: to her he is no lamb but a wolf in police uniform, and she had always known that one day someone would come to expose her terrible secret. Her nightmare has come true; the authorities have finally invaded her home, searching for damning proof. The sight of Ida's unconcealed terror fills the lamb with wolfish potency, and out of the depth of his yearnings for home something "savage," "feverish," "tough" and "starving" begins to swell. Some of these adjectives appear here in juxtaposition to their opposites: "savage homesickness," "feverish bitterness"—combinations that have both an element of oxymoron and an element of synthesis. Later on in the description more and more oxymorons appear, originating from the internal logic of this paradoxical scene.

When he enters the room, Gunther recognizes several objects that attest to the existence of an adolescent boy, including a photograph of Nino. Since he is unable to get an answer to his questions (he has managed to learn only four words of Italian, and the widow does not know a single word of German), he guesses that the woman has a son. And so he is overwhelmed with angry jealousy of the boy who is not yet of conscription age and could "God-damn-it" enjoy himself at home with his mother! And "screw-ing and every-thing—everything!" This is still the envy of a boy distant from his mother for a boy who hangs onto his mother's apron strings, but within this jealousy are incipient sparks of sexual jealousy, of violent sexual frustration, with a sharp Oedipal twist. And, next to Nino's rumpled bed, Gunther's searching eyes suddenly meet the notion of rape: "a thriller showing a half-naked lady on the cover screaming, threatened by a huge, apelike hand." Gunther does not yet know it, but it is already destined to occur. As for Ida:

The soldier's fantastic movements were converted, for Ida, into the precise movements of a fatal machine which was printing also Nino's name beside her own in the blacklist of Jews and their hybrids. As the minutes passed, her own misconceptions were acquiring an obsessive power over her, reducing her to the native, ingenuous terror of a prerational age. Standing, motionless, her coat still on and her little mourning hat on her head, she was no longer a lady of San Lorenzo, but a desperate Asiatic migratory bird, with brown feathers and black crest, overwhelmed in its temporary clump of bushes by a horrendous Occidental deluge.

And thus, while Gunther is, in Ida's eyes, far from being just a child awash in forlorn yearnings, she takes him for a fatal Jew-exposing machine. At the same time, Ida is, in Gunther's eyes, both a longed-for surrogate mother and a bird trapped in the palm of his hand. He turns to the surrogate mother, like a well-bred child, and presents himself courteously: "Mein Name ist Gunther." And he waits, "discontented," because he has expected that the saying of his name will be received as a gesture of placation and will be answered, at the very least, with some small token of affection. If Ida had been able to perceive this vulnerable, infantile bundle of placation, irritability and Oedipal trembling, if she had only responded with a word of affection or courtesy, the rape would have become impossible. But Ida is too frightened to notice. "The lady's eyes, hostile and dazed, merely blinked briefly, suspiciously at those

Germanic sounds, whose only meaning for her was a sibylline threat." What is the reaction to a look of hostility and consternation on the part of someone who will, in less than five minutes, become a brutal rapist? He pulls from his pocket a family photograph, a group picture with his mother in the center, as though signaling to Ida that this is what he so desperately needs now. Ida gives the picture a "frozen" glance, and the embarrassed boy goes on, as though revealing his last card, speaking the name of his hometown (ironically it is Dachau, but the year is only 1941, so that for Ida Ramundo—as for most people—the name still means nothing).

His tone of voice, in uttering that name, was the same that a three-month-old kitten might have, claiming its basket. And for that matter, the name meant nothing to Ida. . . . However, at that innocuous and indifferent name, the wild, transitory migrant, now identified with her heart, leaped inside her. And fluttering horribly in the distorted space of the little room, it began to slam, in chirping tumult, against the walls that had no exit.

Ida's body had remained inert, like her consciousness, with no movement but a throb of the muscles and a defenseless gaze of extreme repulsion, as if she were facing a monster. And at that same moment, the soldier's eyes . . . filled with an innocence almost frightening in its timeless antiquity. . . . To those eyes her gaze seemed the definitive insult. And instantaneously a tempest of anger clouded them. And yet through this clouding there filtered a childish questioning, which no longer expected the sweetness of an answer, but wanted one all the same.

It was at this point that Ida, without thinking, began to shout: "No! No! No!" in the hysterical voice of an immature girl.

Even these screams of hers are not in fear of rape (which still, a moment before it happens, does not enter her mind), but in fear of an approaching epileptic fit. The careful rendering of the last moment before the crime likens the rapist, touchingly, to "a three-month-old kitten," and his victim to a panicked bird; Gunther's eyes still reflect "a childish questioning" (Am I loved, at least a little bit?), and Ida's scream of "No! No! No!" expresses the hysteria of an "immature girl" (both of them are, therefore, "babes," just as in the book's epigraph from Luke, "Thou hast hid these things from the wide and prudent, and hast revealed them unto babes"). The astonished soldier is still in an oxymoronic state, expressed in his look of "innocence almost frightening."

Out of this very same innocence evil now bursts: just like the epileptic fit that has gripped Ida (Gunther cannot even guess what it is), so the fit of evil grips Gunther in an oxymoronic grasp expressed in the words "bitter tenderness."

Unexpectedly, the bitter tenderness that had humiliated him with its torture since that morning was unleashed in him, with a fierce determination! ". . . fare amore! . . . FARE AMORE! . . ." he shouted, repeating in a boyish outburst another two of the 4 Italian words that, in his foresight, he had made them teach him at the frontier. And without even taking off his uniform, caring nothing that she was old, he hurled himself on top of her, throwing her on that disheveled daybed, and raping her with rage as if he wanted to murder her.

He felt her writhe horribly, but, unaware of her illness, he thought she was struggling against him, and he became the more obstinate for this reason, like all drunken soldiery. . . . And he was so charged with stern, repressed tensions that, at the moment of orgasm, he emitted a great scream above her. Then, in the following moment, he peeped at her in time to see her face, filled with amazement, relax in a smile of ineffable humility and sweetness.

"Carina carina," he started saying to her (this was the fourth and last Italian word he had learned). And at the same time he began kissing her, with little kisses full of sweetness, on the dazed face that seemed to look at him and continued smiling at him with a kind of gratitude. Meanwhile, she was gradually coming to, abandoned beneath him. And in a state of relaxation and calm that always passed between the spell and consciousness, she felt him again penetrating her, but slowly this time, with a heart-rending and possessive movement, as if they were already kin and accustomed to each other. She found again the sense of fulfillment and repose she had known as a girl, at the end of an attack . . . but that childish experience of hers was extended today, through her half-waking state, into the blissful sensation of returning to her own, complete body. That other body, greedy, harsh, and warm, which explored her in the center of her maternal sweetness, was, at once, all the hundred thousand fevers and coolnesses and adolescent hungers that flowed together from their jealous lands to fill to the brim of her girlish river. . . . Then it slumped down, becoming once more a sole imploring flesh, dissolving within her womb in a sweet, warm, ingenuous surrender, which made her smile, moved, like the only gift of a poor man, or a child.

It wasn't, for her, not even this time, a true erotic pleasure. It was an extraordinary happiness without orgasm, as sometimes happens in dreams, before puberty.

The soldier, this time, in sating himself, let out a little moan, among light kisses, and letting his whole body sink on her, he promptly fell asleep. . . . The boy slept serenely, snoring . . . and his features, even in his sleep, assumed a grimace of possession and jealousy, like a real lover.

The first rape is violent and hateful, done "with rage as if he wanted to murder her . . . like all drunken soldiers." Yet it is worth noting that the soldier's eyes showed "a childish questioning" before the moment of attack, when he "hurled himself" on his victim, and then satisfied not an overflowing sexual urge but an explicitly murderous urge to vengeance for the insult he had suffered (he had come asking for motherly love and been rejected). His violence is also a reaction to the miserable weakness and submissiveness of the victim (like a bird fluttering in a hunter's hand), and to the violation of the ancient Oedipal taboo (Gunther masters his "mother" with seminal force on her adolescent son's bed).

After the first orgasm there is a moment of Christian grace between the murderer and his victim—a grace that results not from forgiveness but, paradoxically, like the evolution of the rape itself, from utter blindness toward the other: from the days of her childhood, Ida's moment of return from the epileptic fit was always accompanied by an involuntary grimace that looked like a smile of submission and sweetness but was in fact not a smile at all. It was an automatic slackening of jaw muscles that had contracted during the fit. (Earlier there is mention of five-year-old Ida's "smile" as she recovers from an epileptic episode: ". . . that smile, really, was only a physical illusion, produced by her muscles' natural distention after their harsh tautness."

This mirage of a smile, this smileless smile, is sufficient to move the spent Gunther from brutality to the familiar male arrogance. This conceit arouses in him the illusion that he has achieved his first wish, which preceded the crime, before the "hunt," before the morning's insults at the restaurant and at Ida's apartment: "Here, see how much Mother loves you, and how can one not love a cute sweetheart like you?"

At this moment the brutal rapist is transformed into a tender rapist, a loving rapist, an infant of a rapist. But just as his release was more the release of evil urges than a sexual release, so, too, the physical tranquillity that Ida experiences now is not the result of sexual release (she had no orgasm), but the deep unwinding feeling that follows the epileptic fit. Now, after the second, delicate, rape, she notices that the sleepy boy's "brow furrowed in concentration, below the clumps of hair, darker than his lashes, smooth, suggesting a cool, damp softness, like the coat of a little brown kitten just bathed by its mother." And thus the outburst of cruelty and violence ends with a symbolic gesture of motherly, Christian, forgiving grace. The brutal rapist, the soldier who will die in three days' time, now cleansed of his agonies and purged of the evil in him, dozes curled up in the "virgin's" bosom after she has granted him (in retrospect) "the single gift of a pauper or of a child."

Not for nothing, but, rather, out of some mysterious prescience has this childish, cruel German soldier asked to be taught how to say four words in Italian: "Signorina," "fare amore," "carina carina."

All of this is a far cry from the bloody conspiratorial picture placed before the reader in the first opening contract of *La Storia,* but it is not unconnected to the contract that precedes the first one, that which flickers in the epigraphs: the words of a survivor of Hiroshima and St. Luke's words about the children. Indeed, the concept the author offers in order to weld her Christian sentiments to her leftist beliefs seems to break apart in the rape scene: Yes, were it not for Hitler and Mussolini and imperialism and capitalism and colonialism and all of the other forces of darkness and reaction, the innocent Gunther would not have met the pure Ida (and consequently Useppe, the image of the young Jesus, would not have been born). But it was not Hitler and Mussolini who released the monster out of sweet Gunther's depths. The monster was not, after all, a political or a historical or an ideological monster.

In the same deep hiding place from which love, mercy, tenderness, and innocent childish sins flow lurks, too, waiting for its opportunity, the monster of evil, hatred, Oedipal violence and rape-as-murder. This monster is subject, just like grace and mercy, to the truth unspoken by St. Luke in the epigraph.

This, ultimately, is the inner, theological, concealed contract between Elsa Morante's passion-mysteria novel and the reader who is willing to go for it.

How Was It Possible for a Cow to Get onto the Balcony

On the Beginning of
Gabriel García Márquez's Novel
The Autumn of the Patriarch

At the beginning of Gabriel García Márquez's novel *The Autumn of the Patriarch,* a mob invades the presidential palace. The narrator, who is one of the mob, describes how the horde finds the body of the Patriarch, who has ruled the country for hundreds of years, if not forever.

Like the beginning of "A Country Doctor" and the beginning of *Mikdamot,* the beginning of *The Autumn of the Patriarch* seeks to be read, ideally, as one long, uninterrupted sentence; furthermore, although the novel is divided into six sections of tens of pages each, it is not divided into paragraphs—as if told in one long breath. Nor is there a story line in this novel, but, rather, an ebb and flow between the days of the Patriarch's reign and the death of a tyrant who had made time stand still. The beginning is the end: the death of the tyrant and the fall of his regime have occurred not because time has passed, but because time has rotted; it has disintegrated into "the uncountable time of eternity" (and with these words the book concludes). Right from the beginning, the reader is asked, as for a journey to a black hole in outer space, to synchronize his watch to time-out-of-time. Moreover, although the novel is written in the past tense, we eventually discover that the past is not only what was but also what is and what will be. Its movement is more like the disassembling of a Russian nest of dolls than a drill that cuts through various layers. The beginning of the second section makes it clear that the death of the tyrant and the discovery of his body are not just a onetime event marking the end of an era but a reoccurence of a cyclic event.

This dead tyrant is not the heir of or the replacement for the dead tyrant in the beginning of the novel. He is the very same one, he himself (unless one of them is a double; but the double is the tyrant himself in every way). "We" continue to be "we" even though "none of us was old enough to remember what had happened the first time." And in the beginning of the third section: "That was how they found him on the even of his autumn . . . and that was how we found him again many years later . . ."; and again in the beginning of the sixth section: "There he was, then, as if it had been he even thought it might not be, lying on the banquet table. . . ."

The beginning is the conclusion: the present, the event of finding the body, blends and contains both future and past. The moment is eternity. The tyrant does not die after a life spanning several generations, but lives and dies and lives intermittently, and, in fact, not even intermittently: he is alive and dead at every moment, he is himself and not himself, because every moment is eternity and because within the frozen eternity there is only one single thing that goes on incessantly: a continuous process of decay.

This provides for a fascinating paradox: here is a written text that strives to surmount its fundamental nature: to cease to be a line of words, written and read, one after another; to overcome the intrinsic linear essence of time. The reader is asked to move without moving, or to move within the nonmovement, just like the movement of the mob in the halls of the dead palace.

The narrator sounds as if he is widely versed in the history of the palace and of previous ages, capable of tying every rusty carriage and every crumbling coach to its historical or mythical time. But how can he know, for example, that the slit trench in the yard was shared by concubines and soldiers? To what extent does the opening contract demand that the reader trust this narrator?

Time, neglect and degeneration suffuse the opening pages just as they fill the rest of the novel. The mob did fantasize about violently breaking into "the vast lair of power," of attacking the walls or knocking the main door off its hinges with oxbows, but in the end there was no violent revolution, only a gentle, almost dreamlike penetration; the main door opened "with just the push of a voice." Congealed time rules this story, just as it rules the palace, from the very first sentence: ". . . the vultures got into the presidential palace . . . and the flapping of their wings stirred up the stagnant time inside. . . ." The intruders sense that they have entered, not a building, but ages that have congealed while advancing softly into "another age," or a still more ancient silence. They encounter the font in which more than five generations have been christened, and ancient stables, and a berlin from the "stirring days," a wagon "from the time of the plague," and other artifacts covered with cobwebs, each of which marks a period rather than a place.

The time that reigns inside "the vast lair of power" is degenerative time, malodorous, rank with the stench of breeding, charged with damp vapors of effluent propagation. The palace discharges a "warm, soft breeze" of "rotting grandeur" toward the city. The walls are "crumbling." The rosebushes, under which lepers had once slept, are "lunar-dust-covered," and their scent "mingled with the stench . . . and the stink of the henhouse and the smell of dung and urine ferment. . . ." The growth of the garden is "asphyxiating," the clothes "rotting in the sun" near the "open slit trench." Inside, the intruders will discover that the cows have made the halls their own, and the smell of their excrement among the wreckage of the furnishings mixes with the reek of putrefaction emanating from the vultures' bodies. In "an office hidden in the wall" lies the body of the tyrant—the source of various stenches that blow from the palace and overwhelm the city.

What then must the reader take upon himself as a sort of entrance ticket to the palace-cum-cowshed? Must he accept at face value the precise, naturalistic detail, the smells, the crumbling objects, the cow dung and the unresolved briefs as evidence of the seemingly documentary nature of this description? Or else take it all as virtual reality? Or as myth?

Like the opening page of Gogol's "The Overcoat" and the first pages of Kafka's *The Castle,* so too the opening pages of *The Autumn of the Patriarch* lock no doors. One can take it as a description, indeed a grotesque description written in a fantastical-Latin temper, of the people's taking over the palace after the death of an aged ruler in some banana republic that is rife with cruelty and corruption. Or one might just as well read it as an artistic version of an anarchist manifesto decrying the corruption of all regimes, rendering, in vivid colors, the degeneration of all ruling elites. A reading of this sort is liable to miss the metaphysical or theological dimension of *The Autumn of the Patriarch*. Let us not forget that the monstrous dictator is immortal. His death is not an end. Again and again the mob breaks into his quarters, again and again they find the corpse, which the vultures have pecked, again and again he rules supreme, is ever-present, tortures his subjects—or grants them inscrutable and unpredictable favors.

The emissaries of Kafka's castle, sly, dubious creatures, reach the man awaiting an interview, mercilessly ridicule and torment him, but this man will never obtain entrance to the castle or meet its master. In contrast, *The Autumn of the Patriarch* opens with an invasion of the lord's castle, with the discovery of his dead body, but here—as in Kafka and, to some extent, as in Gogol—one cannot touch power itself, but can, at best, touch its tattered and sullied emissaries, its sickening representatives, its opaque, absurd cruelty. As for the ruler himself, ". . . no mortal had ever seen him since the days of the black vomit and yet we knew that he was there, we knew it because the world went on, life went on, the mail was delivered. . . ."

This is not Nietzsche's "death of God," but the disintegration of time; not an apocalyptic end of the world, but a cycle of everlasting decomposition to which the ruler is subject no less than his lowliest subject: ". . . but even then we did not dare believe in his death because it was the second time he had been found in that office. . . . The first time they found him . . . still he governed as if he knew he was predestined never to die. . . ."

Everything stinks and crumbles but nothing ceases. The mob's entry into the palace is no more than a quixotic victory, because the "enemy" is no more than an actor whose role has been precast in a play whose performance begins anew each time the curtain rises.

Nevertheless, the opening contract invites the reader into neither a morbid vale of despair nor a gloomy metaphysical allegory. On the contrary, the beginning is an invitation to a sensuous carnival. García Márquez paints the horror of the inferno in the decayed government house in shades of joyous scandal.

> . . . one January afternoon we had seen a cow contemplating the sunset from the presidential balcony, just imagine, a cow on the balcony of the nation, what an awful thing, what a shitty country, and all sorts of conjectures were made about how it was possible for a cow to get onto a balcony since everybody knew that cows can't climb stairs, and even less carpeted ones, so in the end we never knew if we had really seen it or whether we had been spending an afternoon on the main square and as we strolled along had dreamed that we had seen a cow on the presidential balcony where nothing had been seen or would ever be seen again for many years. . . .

The voice of this impersonal narrator, one of the crowd, who always speaks of "we," is an exultant voice, taking pleasure in the exposure of the disgraced nakedness of presidential grandeur. With every scandalous discovery, with every astounding detail, with every incredible revelation about the life of the powerful, this voice becomes more and more playfully joyous. It even invites the reader to participate in an orgy of blasphemy, in an iconoclastic carnival, by breaking into the fortified "holy of holies," in a euphoria that fuses the despicable horror, the absurd, the incredible decomposition of authority, and the burlesque delight of looting and ravishing.

From the very first words of the novel ("Over the weekend the vultures got into the presidential palace by pecking through the screens on the balcony windows"), the reader must accept the rules of the game; the utter removal of the usual line between the respectable and the burlesque; between the horrific and the hilarious; between metaphysical quest and the mirth of tabloid disclosure; between a godlike ruler and an operatic general in a rotten banana republic.

The reader who approaches this novel armed with decoding chisels is likely to miss what the reader who approaches it with wild laughter will find, and the other way around. From the beginning, the reader is expected to move through the novel on two parallel tracks: it is a dark metaphysical fable about the universe and its master, as much as it is a playful, fiercely ruthless piece of anarchic joy: Kafkaesque and carnivalesque at the same time, this farcical novel manages to offer us a cycle of delirious nightmares.

Take It Outside Before I Throw Up

On the Beginning of Raymond Carver's Story "Nobody Said Anything"

Raymond Carver's story "Nobody Said Anything" is included in the collection *Will You Please Be Quiet, Please?*, first published in 1976. It is the tale of a young boy who finds excuses to avoid going to school, remains in his empty house to watch television, goes fishing in a stream, meets a woman who arouses his desire, meets a strange child with buck teeth, and together they catch something that is called Bigfish, share their catch, and the child-narrator brings something home; he finds his parents in the midst of a quarrel, tries to draw their attention to the gift he has brought them, but they turn and yell at him to throw, for Chrissakes, "that goddamn thing" into the garbage. The title of the story is not entirely clarified until the story's end, when it turns out—although it is not stated—that the title refers to the boy's wish to hear a good word from his parents about the booty he has brought. Perhaps he hoped to please them, and thus make them stop quarreling. Perhaps he hoped to win their love. His hope is finally fulfilled, albeit in an ironic manner: when they see the gift he has brought, the parents indeed stop quarreling, but only for a minute. Instead, they unite in scolding him.

Neither hope nor disappointment is written in the story; they lie in the interstices, which the reader is invited to fill.

The opening does not contain any manifestation of feeling or emotion other than the loathing and anger that each member of the family feels toward the others. The opening section is written in short, factual sentences and bits of dialogue.

> I could hear them out in the kitchen. I couldn't hear what they were saying, but they were arguing. Then it got quiet and she started to cry. I elbowed George. I thought he would wake up and say something to them so they would feel guilty and stop. But George is such an asshole. He started kicking and hollering.
>
> "Stop gouging me, you bastard," he said. "I'm going to tell."
>
> "You dumb chickenshit," I said. "Can't you wise up for once? They're fighting and Mom's crying. Listen."
>
> He listened with his head off the pillow. "I don't care," he said and turned over toward the wall and went back to sleep. George is a royal asshole.
>
> Later I heard Dad leave to catch his bus. He slammed the front door. She had told me before he wanted to tear up the family. I didn't want to listen.
>
> After awhile she came to call us for school. Her voice sounded funny—I don't know. I said I felt sick at my stomach. It was the first week in October and I

hadn't missed any school yet, so what could she say? She looked at me, but it was like she was thinking of something else. George was awake and listening. I could tell he was awake by the way he moved in the bed. He was waiting to see how it turned out so he could make his move.

"All right." She shook her head. "I just don't know. Stay home, then. But no TV, remember that."

George reared up. "I'm sick too," he said to her. "I have a headache. He gouged me and kicked me all night. I didn't get to sleep at all."

"That's enough!" she said. "You are going to school, George! You're not going to stay here and fight with your brother all day. Now get up and get dressed. I mean it. I don't feel like another battle this morning."

George waited until she left the room. Then he climbed out over the foot of the bed. "You bastard," he said and yanked all the covers off me. He dodged into the bathroom.

"I'll kill you," I said but not so loud that she could hear.

I stayed in bed until George left for school. When she started to get ready for work, I asked if she would make a bed for me on the couch. I said I wanted to study. On the coffee table I had the Edgar Rice Burroughs books I had gotten for my birthday and my Social Studies book. But I didn't feel like reading. I wanted her to leave so I could watch TV.

On the surface, what we have here is no more than a documentary pile of real-life materials: there are no descriptions of place, no background, no levels of hidden meaning, no emotions, no doubts, no motives, no stream of consciousness, just a stream of trivia: the mother and father are separated by a quarrel, as are the two brothers, who call each other "bastard" and "dumb chickenshit." There is no contact between father and children, and mother emanates suspicion, impatience and rebuke toward her children; the narrator is a deceitful, manipulative child; the brother, George, a snitch and a liar. When the narrator hears from his mother that his father wants to "tear up" the family, his reaction is: "I don't want to listen." George, when he hears his mother's weeping, also reacts: "I don't care," then he goes back to sleep. They all seem to be sick of one another.

Despite all this, one can discern certain nuances: the mother's response to the narrator is less impatient than her response to his brother, and the narrator's response to his mother's suffering is slightly different from George's. When the narrator hears her crying, rather than ignore it he wakes his brother and instigates a little manipulation, trying to push George into saying something that will cause the parents to feel bad, so they will stop fighting, but the scheme fails because George refuses to cooperate.

The reader must fill in the information gaps by himself: in the first lines of the story we do not have "my parents" or "my brother" but only "I could hear them out in the kitchen," "she started to cry," "I elbowed George." Even that it is morning, and that the brothers are sleeping in one bed, is inferred, not stated. The reader's task, to "assemble" the voices in the first paragraph into a family picture, is in preparation for the active role the reader will fill later on. He will have to understand from the child's stream of factual-behavioristic reportage the depth of loneliness, the thirst for love and the desperate attempt to repair relationships that are beyond repair. Even though the words "loneliness," "love" and "repair" never appear, even though it seems that they are not even possible in this dry, matter-of-fact story, the reader's task is to sense them behind the general dreariness.

Hasty reading might leave the impression that the story is no more than a chronological record of the events in a day of a child's life, which lack any organizing principle. Here is a list of the events after the opening paragraph:

The child stays with Mom until she leaves for work. He asks her to make a bed for him on the couch. He lies to her: wanted to study.

He watches television with the sound off. Reads *The Princess of Mars.*

There are several tender moments when the mother and child are alone in the house. Then she goes to work.

The child watches television. Smokes one of his mother's cigarettes. Looks for condoms in their drawers. Finds Vaseline and gets a hard-on.

Afterwards grabs something to eat, writes a note and leaves the house. Goes to Birch Creek. Sees the outside world; it was fall but not cold yet.

Gets a ride with a woman in a red car. ". . . she was sharp enough . . . had a sweater with nice boobs inside" (but also little pimples around her mouth and curlers in her hair). Imagines that she takes him home with her.

The woman lets him out at the crossroads. He continues walking. Imagines her in his bedroom and gets another hard-on.

Gets to the creek. Remembers going fishing with

Dad. Eats the food he brought. Tries to catch something. Again imagines fooling around with the woman in the red car.

Catches a trout. Tries not to think about the woman anymore, but from trying he becomes hard again.

While he is fishing, he remembers that he swore on the Bible to jerk off less, and right after swearing jerked off on that Bible.

Meets a strange kid with buck teeth. The kid has found a huge fish, big as an arm, but can't manage to catch it.

The narrator helps him. Together they manage to catch a long skinny fish, "bigger than anything I had ever caught." Evening. It begins to turn cold.

They carry the fish on a stick between them. They argue how to divvy it up. They compromise. The narrator takes the fish's head.

He parts from the strange kid. Goes home. George is outside on his bike. In the kitchen Mom and Dad are fighting again. She is crying.

The child takes off his boots, intends to march in with a smile on his face and surprise his parents with the gift he has brought them from the stream.

He hears his father say: "What do kids know?" The mother answers, "If I thought that, I'd rather see them dead first."

The frying pan begins to burn. The mother throws it against the wall. The father says, "Have you lost your mind?"

The child enters the kitchen smiling. "You won't believe what I caught. . . ."

The mother yells, "Please . . . take it out before I throw up." And the father screams, "Take that god-damn thing out of here."

The child goes back outside; story ends.

This sequence of occurrences seems to be random and unfocused. The point of view is external, despite the use of the first person; the text is almost behaviorist ("I could tell he was awake by the way he moved in the bed"). Yet a closer reading may reveal a censored internal story, the outlines of a carefully constructed composition. The account begins in the morning, inside the house, and later takes place outside. In the evening, we are once more inside the house, then outside again. Furthermore, the story opens with a failed attempt to distract the parents from their quarrel, and there is another such failed attempt at the story's conclusion.

The child-narrator moves from unrequited courtship of the family (especially of his mother) to sexuality (the search for condoms, the Vaseline, the strange woman and the fantasies she arouses, the thoughts of masturbation) and on to the meeting with the strange kid and the secretive experience of the two boys on the bank of the stream with a "long and skinny" fish, about which the strange kid says, "I want to show him to my dad so bad," and the child-narrator does try to show it to his father that evening.

The description of the two boys dealing with the fish is close to sexual experimentation. The fish "gave a long slow tremble. . . . We looked at him, kept touching him," and later: "I held his big head under the water and opened his mouth. The stream poured into his mouth and out the other end. . . ." After this experimentation, the boy returns home and tries to stop the quarrel between his parents by telling them what has happened to him and by showing them what his adventure has produced. His appeal to his parents may be the only emotional sentence he utters in the whole story:

> "You won't believe what I caught at Birch Creek. Just look. Look here.
> "Look at this. Look what I caught."

Yet the mother does not see a fish. She sees something that scares and disgusts her; she reacts with a shriek of revulsion, as if the child had brought home, not a fish, but, say, a used condom.

> "Oh, oh, my God! What is it? A snake! What is it? Please, please take it out before I throw up."

The child then turns to his father and pleads with him to at least take a look.

> "But look, Dad. Look what it is. . . .
> "There was another one, too," I hurried on. "A green one. I swear! It was green. Have you ever seen a green one?"

The father refuses to take an interest; he joins in the mother's reaction.

> "Take that goddamn thing out of here! . . . throw it in the goddamn garbage!"

But what, in fact, has the child brought from the creek? What did the parents see?

This is the "enigmatic point" that exists in many of Carver's stories, the point at which the reader is invited to return to the beginning of the story and choose: if he wants to believe or not believe in the fish; if he wants to accept or reject the report of the child-narrator who has already been exposed as a liar.

At the end of the story the boy is once again alone, outside. "What was there filled the creel. . . . I held it. I held that half of him."

"Nobody Said Anything" is not a "puritanical" story; it contains implicit expressions as well as graphically explicit descriptions of sexual desires awakening in an adolescent boy. In many literary works of previous generations there was self-righteous censorship of sexual descriptions, alongside a flood of emotional accounts. Here the sexual censorship is replaced by emotional censorship: the child-narrator has no difficulty relating his search for his parents' condoms, does not refrain from reporting when and why he gets an erection, but nowhere in the story does he say "I loved," "I missed" or even "I was insulted," "I was sad." From the very first paragraph the reader is invited to imagine, through this veil of emotion-censorship, not only what the parents saw when they looked at half of a fish, but also—and primarily— what takes place in the interior story: loneliness, compassion for the mother's suffering, pain at the disintegration of the family, vain attempts to talk, fantasies, lack of love and the suppressed torments of adolescence.

From Tnuva* to Monaco

On the Beginning of Yaakov Shabtai's Story
"A Private and Very Awesome Leopard"

Several of the stories in Yaakov Shabtai's collection *Uncle Peretz Takes Off* are told from the perspective of a young boy in Tel Aviv of the 1940s. This boy is the child of a conformist-socialist family. He observes in amazement his ultraorthodox grandfather, his grandmother, who lives in a sort of Eastern European shtetl enclave she creates for herself, and several eccentric, grotesque or bohemian uncles who reject the constricting conventions of the Zionist-socialist class. Each one of these uncles is, in his own way, the black sheep of the family.

The child's secret fascination with "nonconformists" is the result of a vague sense of claustrophobia and repulsion. Although the family home is at the center of this collection of stories, it is barely described; instead, it is

---

* Tnuva was a once-popular chain of inexpensive cooperative dairy restaurants in Israel.

sketched by contrasts and opposites, by the ostracized uncles, and through the self-righteous indignation the "dangerous" uncles evoke in the family. The home itself is "proper," "puritan," awash in proletarian platitudes and clichés. It is in the best tradition of Zionist socialism at its worst.

In most of the stories, the narrator is too young to take a conscious stand toward his "home." Only in his later, great, novels, *Zichron D'varim* and *Sof Davar*, does Shabtai engage in a comprehensive and penetrating stocktaking of his parents' world: he reconstructs it with depth and breadth, ferociously condemning its hypocrisy and tyranny, its castrating effect on the life of its offspring, yet he longs for it and laments its disappearance.

Several of the stories in *Uncle Peretz Takes Off* are told from a complex perspective, blending the amazed innocence of the sensitive boy with the awareness of an ironical adult. Often there is no explicit dividing line between the child's observations and the adult's recollections, as though the two voices are telling one story, and the reader is invited to enjoy the wealth of fine modulations between the two points of view; for example, in the opening sentences of the story from which the collection takes its name:

> Uncle Peretz was no uncle. He was a Communist, and except for my grandmother everyone said he would turn out badly. His father turned his back on him out of insult and disappointment, and the rest of the family also kept their distance from him.

From the paradox in the first sentence, we gather—although it is not stated anywhere—that the speaker is a mere boy, but the third sentence is based on a reconstructed reflection. In contrast to the beginning of *Mikdamot*, this is not an attempt to conjure up a primal experience with the tools of existing language; it is a subtle blend of what the child had understood and what the narrator had realized much later.

The beginning of "A Private and Very Awesome Leopard" also employs such a blend, although less explicitly:

> I have an uncle in Monaco, but there have been rumors lately that he moved to Lisbon and there, or near there, established a farm to breed fighting cocks. The most recent solid report about him came three years ago. Aunt Idel from Buffalo, my grandmother's phantom sister, informed us in one of her letters that her son, Philip, who owns a big jewelry store in Beverly Hills, thought he might have seen this uncle of mine hurrying across a street in San Francisco.
>
> The report caused no reaction in our family. It was filed in frozen silence just as my uncle's name was always filed and erased since the last time he left the country, leaving behind a sediment of shame and anger in addition to two fair-haired children, four wives, a desperate band of creditors, a moth-eaten pile of suits and top hats, a mournful Great Dane and one calling card in the keeping of his childhood friend, the painter Edmond Rubin. On this calling card were printed, in gold lettered flourishes, his full name and titles: 'Albert Albert Avram Joachim Emmanuel Weiss. Doctor of Jurisprudence, Doctor of Economics, Expert.'
>
> That was seven years ago on a winter's day.
>
> When he first arrived in the country, four years after the war ended, the whole family put on their best clothes and went by taxi with a bouquet of gladio-

luses to Uncle Noah's house. Relatives, acquaintances and some of his former townsmen were already gathered there. Aunt Shoshanna . . . served tea and poppyseed cookies.

Everyone drank tea, engaged in small talk and peered into the street. They were all waiting for the refugee.

At precisely seven o'clock the doorbell rang.

"It's Pinek!" called Uncle Noah and everyone hurried into the hall.

"I'm here!" declared Pinek, standing in the doorway.

The story begins in the present tense: "I have an uncle in Monaco," and ends in the present: "And now I have an uncle in Monaco." Presumably one could not easily figure when this present occurs: Uncle first appears on the family stage as a refugee from Europe "four years after the war." Thus it is 1949. Between the uncle's first and second comings there is a lapse of half a year; the adventures of his "second coming" take about two years, accounting for the busy months following the press conference, the change of seasons, and several other milestones mentioned in the affair of the circus; afterward he disappears for several months, and "returns for the High Holy Days." He again sojourns in the country intermittently, for at least several months: summer has ended, winter has come, Aunt Tsirle and her children also arrive. And with their arrival, the uncle retreats for a while from the vanities of this world: "For almost a year my uncle punished . . . the world," and for several more weeks made feverish preparations to conquer Monaco, and then up and disappeared. That was "seven years ago." Between the uncle's first appearance (in '49) and his disappearance, four or five

years have passed. And another seven years passed between his disappearance and the telling of the story ("Now
I have an uncle in Monaco"). A cautious estimate therefore brings us to the conclusion that the story is being told
in 1960 or 1961.

Even if the child who recalls all the details of Uncle
Pinek's first disappearance was very young at the time of
this premiere performance, "now"—at the time when he
relates the chronicles of the uncle from Monaco—he is
no longer young, maybe no longer a child. Yet in the tone
of the story there is no sense of earlier or later: throughout, there is an omniscient, ironic narrator, a mind reader
whose voice interweaves with the voice of the conform-
ing, naïve, mooning child. Nonetheless, from the "under-
ground broadcasts" that flicker intermittently below the
surface of the story, there are sometimes bursts of understanding that the child witness was surely incapable of,
due to his age, his innocence and his puritan family censorship: family scandals are not discussed in front of the
children, and dirty linen is not washed in view of the
younger generation.

If we try to translate the opening paragraphs into another language, we will discover that the task is virtually
impossible, not because of linguistic complexity—the language is simple and straightforward—but because of the
array of connotations connecting the most intimate codes
of the Ashkenazi working or lower middle class. The
roots of this class are in Eastern Europe, but there is always an Aunt Idel in Buffalo and a cousin named Philip
who sells jewelry in Beverly Hills. (A text suffused with
such codes is, like poetry, particularly hard to translate,
because it functions rather like a family joke: you mention to someone in the family "Auntie Gita's potato pan-

cakes," and the whole family bursts into laughter while a stranger sits dumbfounded.)

A sharp comic dissonance is created at the beginning of the story when the reader is invited to shift his glance from common Eastern European Jewish geography to the exotic geography in which the uncle's mysterious figure floats: from the court of the princes of Monaco to Aunt Idel's house in Buffalo, from the cock farm in Lisbon to the jewelry store in Beverly Hills, from the accursed Faustian Uncle Albert Albert Avram Joachim Emmanuel Weiss to his brother Noah's Tnuva Workers' Dairy Cooperative, and to Aunt Shoshanna fixing scrambled eggs and salad.

The narrator positions himself in the beginning of the story with the phrase "in our family"—namely, he belongs to the clan that ostracizes the uncle and files "in frozen silence" the latest "solid report" about him. (In fact, the "solid report" is that Cousin Philip "thought he might have seen" this uncle hurrying across a street in San Francisco.) Furthermore: the narrator takes his stand, by inference, on the side of the tribal, righteous values— for instance, when he feels the need to brag that Cousin Philip's jewelry store is "big."

And yet the very plot of the story, the very fact that the embarrassing uncle is at the center of the stage, is itself a subversive act, breaking the conspiracy of silence the family has imposed on the scoundrel.

The narrator counts the inventory the uncle left behind. This catalogue, which includes—in the same breath—objects, people, hurt feelings and a dog, recalls the inventory in the poor room of Yakov Ivanov, nicknamed Bronze, in "Rothschild's Fiddle"; there too we find an indiscriminate accounting of the stove, the miserable furnishings, the wife, Marfa, and some work tools.

But in Chekhov's story the jumble of souls and objects is meant to attest to Bronze's vulgarity, while in "A Private and Very Awesome Leopard" it indicates the viewpoint of a wide-eyed child.

Both the inventory left by the uncle and the form and content of his calling card are evidence, at least as far as the family is concerned, of an extravagant, bohemian, fraudulent character. Moreover, every item included in the "estate" and every title inscribed on the calling card constitutes a scandalous provocation against Zionist-socialist values. A person who "defects" from the country and leaves behind him "shame and anger" also leaves a stain on the honor of the entire family; "two fair-haired children, four wives" are a desecration of the puritan code; "a desperate band of creditors" is striking evidence of frivolousness and financial irresponsibility; "suits and top hats" are an insult to the ethos of the open-collar-tieless-shirt society; a dog is a Gentile delight; a calling card embellished with gold letters is a remnant of the bourgeois "old world," and also a syndrome of dubious wheeling-dealing *luftgescheften*.

The outrage that infuriates the family but secretly enchants the child swells as the story evolves. As family, acquaintances and former townsmen gather at the home of Aunt Shoshanna and Uncle Noah to greet the "refugee," a survivor of the flames of Europe, it turns out that the newcomer is not at all a wretched "relic." Rather, he turns out to be a portly proprietor, a rich man of sorts, full of pleasantries and mannerisms, kissing ladies' hands, and concluding in Yiddish: "Tomorrow I am seeing your Minister of Finance." Isn't the Jewish Diaspora supposed to be "desiccated and vitiated," as the saying goes? But here it is personified by gleeful Uncle Pinek, not at all vitiated, not in the least desiccated, but even presuming to look down at the Zionist-socialist wing of the family.

Moreover, an uncle dressed in a suit, "his cuffs and necktie fastened with gold pins," who distributes small gifts and calling cards to the family members, not only represents an arrogant provocation to the world of Tnuva, but also embodies everyone's censored, repressed desires, the petit-bourgeois appetites manifested by the gladioluses. The working-class family gathered under the "picture of Berl Katznelson"—éminence grise of the workers' movement—has put on "their best clothes" for the occasion, and arrived at the fete "by taxi," a spread of tea and cookies has been laid, and vases filled with fresh flowers. "The china and silver, specially taken out of the breakfront, gleamed in the lamplight"—it was almost, perhaps, like the house of the prosperous cousin Philip, owner of the big jewelry store beyond the sea.

Yaakov Shabtai's uncles' world intersects here with the cruel world of the contemporary Israeli playwright Hanoch Levin. Uncle Pinek, disguised as Señor Albert Albert Avram Joachim Emmanuel Weiss, "careerist," hedonist, *luftmentsch* and imposter, is not just the terror and disgrace of the family; he is also the incarnation of its forbidden dreams. He is momentarily able to enchant them with his fantasies, which are populated with grand earthshaking enterprises and audacious pioneering initiatives.

The Ashkenazi Jewish shtetl was and is no more. Its traces can be found all the way from the local branch of Tnuva to Buffalo and Beverly Hills. Its dreary sons and daughters had created a spartan state on the Biblical hills of Canaan or else ended up in Lisbon, erecting a "farm for the breeding of fighting cocks." All of them, openly or secretly, yearn to be like the shtetl big shot. The shtetl big shot does not actually appear in "A Private and Very Awesome Leopard," but without the presence of his shadow it is hard to grasp the secret desires of the Tel Aviv branch of the family. Or the connection between Tel Aviv and the American branch. Or the relations between both of these branches and the black-sheep brother who has returned from the dead, Joseph the Dreamer, the one who leaves in discord only to achieve greatness in alien lands and to bring prosperity and honor to himself and to the brothers who disowned him.

The child narrator in "A Private and Very Awesome Leopard" does not invite the reader to discover that the emperor is naked. On the contrary, he captivates the reader with a wealth of disguises, concealed behind the puritan principles, hidden behind a bounty of ever-changing calling cards.

Conclusion

Leisurely Pleasure

Newspaper advertisements seduce some of us into taking all kinds of speed-reading courses: in return for a small fee, we are promised that we will be taught how to save valuable time, how to read five pages per minute, how to scan the page horizontally, how to skip the details and to reach the bottom line speedily. The suggestions that have been presented in this volume, ten glances into the opening contracts of ten novels or stories, may serve as the introduction to a course in slow-reading: the pleasures of reading, like other delights, should be consumed in small sips.

Once, when we were in sixth or seventh grade, the school nurse entered our classroom, heroically enclosed herself with thirty boys and exposed the facts of life. This nurse was amazingly daring; she fearlessly showed us systems and their functions, drew on the blackboard maps of the reproductive plumbing, described all the physical

equipment and clarified all the attachments. She spared us
nothing, eggs and sperm, membranes and mechanics. She
then went on to give us the real horror show, chilling our
blood with descriptions of the twin monsters lying at the
gates of sex: Pregnancy and Venereal Disease. Stunned and
cowed, we left the classroom two hours later. The child I
was then understood, more or less, what was supposed to
go into where and what was supposed to receive what,
and what sort of awful disasters could befall me, but that
child has no understanding of why any sane person would
want to get caught in this dragon's lair in the first place.
It turned out that the energetic nurse, who had no hesita-
tion about revealing every last detail, from hormones to
glands, nonetheless skipped over a marginal detail: she did
not tell us, did not even hint, that these complex proce-
dures entailed, at least occasionally, some pleasure. Perhaps she thought that in not doing so, she would make
our innocent young lives safer. Perhaps she had no idea.

And this is precisely what some of the literati are doing
to us: they analyze everything ad nauseam, techniques,
motifs, oxymorons and metonyms, allegory and conno-
tation, hidden Jewish allusions, latent psychological keys
and sociological implications, and archetypal characters
and fateful ideas and whatnot. Only the pleasure of reading do they castrate—just a bit—so it doesn't get in the
way; so that we remember that literature is not playing
games, and, in general, that life is no picnic.

Yet Gogol's nose and Yizhar's orange hue and the cow
on the balcony and Yaakov Shabtai's uncles, and even
Kafka's diabolical horses—all of them, in addition to providing the well-known delicatessen of education, information, and so on, lure us into a world of pleasures and joyous
games. In every one of these stories we are permitted some-

thing that is not allowed "outside": not just a reflection of our familiar world and not just a journey into the unknown, but also the very fascination with touching the "inconceivable." Whereas, inside a story, it becomes conceivable, accessible to our senses and our fears, to our imagination and our passions.

The game of reading requires you, the reader, to take an active part, to bring to the field your own life experience and your own innocence, as well as caution and cunning. The opening contracts are sometimes hide-and-seek and sometimes Simon Says and sometimes more like a game of chess. Or poker. Or a crossword puzzle. Or a prank. Or an invitation into a maze. Or an invitation to dance. Or a mocking courtship that promises but does not deliver, or delivers the wrong goods, or delivers what it had never promised or delivers just a promise.

And ultimately, like any contract, if you do not read the fine print you may be taken for a ride; but sometimes you may be taken for a ride precisely by getting bogged down in the fine print and failing to see the forest for the trees.

Every day, my mailbox drowns in invitations to lecture before all sorts of conferences and symposia about "The Image of the Israeli-Arab Conflict in Literature" or "The Reflection of the Nation in the Novel" or "Literature as a Mirror of Society." But if all you want is to look in a mirror, why read books?

Once upon a time, on a nudist beach, I saw a man sitting, naked, delightedly engrossed in an issue of *Playboy*.

Just like that man, on the inside, not on the outside, is where the good reader ought to be while reading.

Permissions

Effi Briest by Theodore Fontane, translated by Douglas Parmee (Penguin Classics, 1967). Copyright © Douglas Parmee, 1967. Reproduced by permission of Penguin Books Ltd.

"In the Prime of Her Life," *At the Handle of the Lock* by S. Y. Agnon (Schocken Publishing House Ltd., Tel Aviv). English translation copyright © by The Institute for the Translation of Hebrew Literature.

"The Nose," *Complete Tales of Nikolai Gogol* (University of Chicago Press, 1985; translated by Constance Garnett). Copyright © The Estate of Constance Garnett.

"A Country Doctor," *Stories: 1904–1924,* translated by J. A. Underwood (London and Sydney: MacDonald & Co., 1981). Reproduced by permission of Little Brown.

"Rothschild's Fiddle," *The Stories of Anton Chekhov,* Robert N. Linscott, ed. (New York: Modern Library, 1932) Reproduced by permission of Random House, Inc.

Mikdamot by S. Yizhar. English language translation by Maggie Bar-Tura ©. Reprinted by permission of Henry Holt and Company, Inc.

History: A Novel by Elsa Morante, trans., William Weaver. Translation copyright © 1977 by Alfred A. Knopf, Inc. Reprinted by permission of the publisher. © Elsa Morante Estate. Published in Italy by Guilio Einaudi Editore, Torino.

"Nobody Said Anything," *Will You Please Be Quiet, Please?* by Raymond Carver © copyright 1976 Tess Gallagher.

"A Private and Very Awesome Leopard," *Uncle Peretz Takes Off* by Yaakov Shabtai. Copyright © by Yaakov Shabtai's Estate. English language translation copyright © by The Institute for the Translation of Hebrew Literature.